HISTORY OF BIBLICAL CHRISTIANITY

AN INTRODUCTORY STUDY OF BEGINNING CHRISTIANITY AND THE NEW TESTAMENT

HAP C.S. LYDA

21ST CENTURY PRESS
FORT WORTH

HISTORY OF BIBLICAL CHRISTIANITY:
AN INTRODUCTORY STUDY OF BEGINNING CHRISTIANITY AND THE NEW TESTAMENT

Third Printing 2008

Printed in the United States of America
21st Century Press, POB 93149, Southlake, Texas 76092-1149

Design by Lance E. Lyda, Camenae Group, Inc.

Printing by Hanson Printing

Library of Congress Catalog Number BR162.3.L93 2007
ISBN 0-9630629-6-4

Library of Congress Cataloging-in-Publication Data

Lyda, Hap C.S., 1932—
History of biblical Christianity: an introductory study of beginning Christianity and the New Testament / Hap C.S. Lyda.
p. cm.
Includes appendices, bibliographical references, and index.
ISBN 0-9630629-6-4 (alk. paper)
1. Church history—Primitive and early church. 2. Christianity—Origin. 3. Bible. N.T.—Criticism, interpretation, etc.
I. Title.
BR162.3.L93 2007
270.1—dc22

2006021620

Contents

Prologue

History of Biblical Christianity is an introductory work. It is a study of the background, founding, and early years of Christianity, and of the literature of the New Testament. It is written at a college/adult level as a beginning study.

The book has Three Parts: Backgrounds, Jesus, and Christianity.

Part I describes the backgrounds that furnish the setting for biblical Christianity: Roman rule, Greek culture, and Jewish religion.

Part II is about Jesus, what we can know about the historical Jesus and what the New Testament Gospel writers thought about him.

Part III traces the development of Christianity/church from its founding through the middle of the second century, especially using the books of the New Testament from The Acts of the Apostles through Revelation.

Following these Three Parts are numerous helps for further appreciation of biblical Christianity:

—The Glossary is extensive.

—The Appendices are a generous eighteen in number. They present in readable and condensed form material seldom if ever gathered in one volume, such as chronologies, festivals, rituals, biographical sketches, population and churches statistics, New Testament analyses, vital points of Christian theology in the biblical era, essential church characteristics, varieties of Christianity in the biblical era, and women named in the New Testament.

—The Bibliography presents an array of works especially relevant to the time period covered by this book.

—The Index is a quick guide to major persons and topics.

This book comes after my having taught Religion and Philosophy courses at the college level for nearly forty years. I write as an historian of religion. I try to describe what actually happened in an objective manner. I look at the material first and then draw conclusions, rather than impose theological biases before looking at the material.

Consequently, this book can be used by persons both within and without Christianity. One may be a believer or a non-believer and still study the history of Christianity during the biblical era for great benefit. Christianity is a huge and ongoing movement. It provides a base for much of Western civilization. Knowledge of its beginning and development is essential for understanding our own heritage, conduct, and destiny. Knowledge of beginning Christianity and the literature of the New Testament is valuable to everyone; to those who make Christianity their religion, it is indispensable.

Do keep in mind that there are difficulties in studying events that are two thousand years old. That was an era before the printing press, modern media, internet, and DVDs. Compounding the study of biblical Christianity is the fact that both Jesus and the earliest Christians expected the order of this world to end and a new Heaven and a new Earth to be established by cataclysmic fiat of God. Thus, there was little need to preserve records at the very first since the whole civilization was going to be reconstituted; when the fiat did not come, then records were begun. This book is based on those records that were preserved through the middle of the second century CE.

Hap C.S. Lyda
Fort Worth, Texas

History of Biblical Christianity

Part I

Backgrounds

Backgrounds

Chapter 1

Backgrounds—Roman

Introduction

The rise of the Christian religion began with Jesus. He was born and raised, and he lived and died in the Jewish provinces of Judea and Galilee in the land variously called Israel, Palestine, or Holy Land, and located on the eastern shore of the Mediterranean Sea.

His land was under the political rule of Rome. Society at large was under the influence of Greek culture. His religious heritage was from the Jews.

In this chapter the Roman background is examined.

Roman Political Rule

The political dominance of Rome was a constant factor in this era of biblical religion. Rome had been founded in the eighth century BCE. It had become the super power of the Mediterranean world during the hundred years before Jesus' birth. It annexed the Jewish provinces into its realm in 63 BCE.

Immediately preceding the annexation the Jews had autonomy under the Jewish Hasmonean dynasty. Just before the year 63 BCE, two of the dynasty brothers vied for the kingship. One of them curried the assistance of Rome in order to secure his position. Rome obliged. General Pompey came to settle the affair, but did so by taking over and annexing the provinces into what would soon become the Roman Empire. (The Jewish provinces usually were four: Judea, Samaria, Galilee, and Perea. Rome sometimes reapportioned these for governing purposes.)

Herod the Great

In 37 BCE Rome appointed Herod as king over the Jewish territory. He appeared to be a wise choice: he was wealthy, handsome, and seemed interested in maintaining Jewish traditions and religion. He was from Idumaea, a nation just to the south of Judea. He was of mixed parentage—Idumaean and Jewish. He moved to be more acceptable to his Jewish constituency by marrying one of the Hasmonean princesses, Miriamne. Apparently he loved her as well as wanting her for political consolidation.

Herod was an able administrator. He was a superb builder of public structures. He began the restoration of the Temple in Jerusalem to more than its Solomonic beauty. He reigned until 4 BCE.

While able, so able that he was given the title "The Great," he also was suspicious, authoritarian, and cruel. He came to suspect Miriamne of wanting to restore the kingship to the Hasmonean family, so he had her and their two sons killed.

He had the authority from Rome to keep the peace—*"Pax Romana"*—by whatever means necessary. He could make arbitrary decisions on the spot to deal with disturbances. He put to immediate death hundreds of disturbers of the peace; on one occasion he crucified approximately three thousand Jews both to keep order and to teach the populace a lesson.

He was cruel in such a way as the killing of the babies—"Slaughtering of the Innocents"—two years old and under when he heard that a new king of the Jews had been born. The Gospel According to Matthew describes his duplicity with the Wise Men from the East in order to determine where this king had been born (although this incident is viewed by some scholars as legendary).

To many Jews, Herod's bad points outweighed his good points. The list of his bad points is lengthy: he took away the crown from the Hasmoneans; he disregarded many Jewish laws; he spent Jewish taxes on Gentile projects; he violated Jewish women as he desired; he killed many

Pharisees in a 6 BCE incident; he had spies whose word he took and executed leading Jews; he appointed and deposed the high priests often; and he was kept in power by Rome, which meant that Jewish resentment extended to Rome because of him. The main Jewish discontent appears to have been the dominance of a foreign power over their provinces. The Jews remembered especially two high points of freedom from dominance in their history: deliverance from bondage in Egypt in the thirteenth century BCE and the successful revolutionary war against the Syrians by the Hasmoneans in the second century BCE. These were made into national festivals of celebration: Pesach, aka Passover, and Chanukkah aka Lights aka Rededication. The Jews resented bondage to any foreign power, including the present power of Rome.

Moreover, the Jews viewed autonomous nationhood as a necessity in their Covenants with God. Abraham had agreed with God on a relationship that contained the clause spoken by God, "I will make of you a great nation." To be under the dominance of any foreign power was not part of the Abrahamic Covenant, according to Jewish interpretation. In spite of the fact that Rome had brought many advantages to its provinces, such as a general condition of peace, constitutional law, and comparatively safe travel, Jews chaffed at subservience to foreign power.

Through the centuries there had been several types of hopes for permanent, independent nationhood. One was getting into a "Promised Land." Another was a legal system that would give equal opportunity to every person. Another was a monarchy "like all the other nations," ruled by a messiah—a king—chosen by God, ruling from a "holy city" with a "holy temple." Still another was individual, heartfelt religion brilliantly described by prophets such as Jeremiah.

None of these hopes materialized into a permanent, ideal society. All of them resulted in disappointment. Consequently, by the time of Jesus there were calls for another mighty intervention by God. The belief was that God could and ought to intervene, either by direct fiat or possibly through another messiah, to establish Israel as a great national and righteous state, an Israel free from any and all foreign domination as well as free from any and all sin. God could and ought to eliminate both foreign rule and unrighteousness in the land. The Romans would be smitten, and a righteous teacher would lead the people to Godliness.

Other Rulers

Following the death of Herod the Great in 4 BCE the Jewish provinces were divided between two of his sons. Herod Antipas was made ruler of Perea and Galilee, 4 BCE-39 CE. Herod Archelaus was placed over Judea and Samaria, but with the lessened title of "ethnarch," a step below "king," 4 BCE-6 CE. Archelaus was as hated by the Jews as his father. Archelaus looted the Temple treasury, aroused rebel bands who were suppressed by Roman forces with quick and great severity, and was so inept that Rome replaced him with a series of governors, variously called "procurator" or "prefect," designations one and two degrees below that of ethnarch. One of these tweaked the antagonism of the Jews by locking up the high priests' vestments and releasing them only on high holy days. There were six different governors until the death of Jesus in 29/30 CE. Pontius Pilate (r. 26-36) was in the governor's chair at the time of Jesus' death.

In the Roman homeland after 63 BCE the leader who emerged was Julius Caesar. He is famous for "crossing the Rubicon" River in 49 BCE which meant that he invaded Rome itself and claimed supreme power. He was brilliant, but behaved like a dictator. Consequently his assassination was plotted and carried out on the Ides (15th) of March in 44 BCE by officials who preferred a republic. The leadership of the budding empire was thrown into chaos until Julius' young nephew, Octavian, began winning internecine battles and popular support. He completed his sweep to power by defeating Antony and Cleopatra at Actium in 31 BCE. He changed Rome from the republic it had been for most of its history into an imperial state. Octavian ruled nearly forever, it seemed, from 31 BCE to 14 CE. He was the ruler at the time of Jesus' birth. His full name was Gaius Julius Caesar Octavianus.

Octavian ordered the seas to be safe for travelers. He directed the building of thousands of miles of roads, primarily for the movement of the military, but also for the convenience of travelers and the promotion of commerce. He amassed great national wealth, built public buildings, aqueducts, baths, stadia, and he patronized the arts and learning.

Octavian was no mean admirer of himself. He allowed himself to be called "Augustus," designating one of magnificence and rank; then "Imperator Caesar divi filius," meaning "son of a deified Julius Caesar"; then "Pontifex Maximus," the chief priest of the old Roman religion; and other titles. The outcome of this titling was that Octavian firmly established a customary way of regarding the ruler as having some measure of the spirit of divinity. It is probable that the ruler was not thought to be an immortal god by most people; yet the general opinion was that the number of gods was fluid, so Octavian could be added to the pantheon in some way without too much ado. Octavian surely knew that it was advantageous to his rule that he be connected to divinity. He expected the people to give him highest respect and was prone to demand it more and more as his very long tenure progressed. This expectation of divine respect was a sore point to the Jews who believed that God—and to the Jews there was only one God, YHWH—did not go about perpetuating himself with heirs on Earth, as some of the traditional gods may have done.

After Christianity began, the status of the Roman ruler also became a tension point for those who believed that Jesus was their Lord and only Lord; they refused to call the Roman ruler "lord," a title he expected to be used in addressing him. When Christians were prosecuted and persecuted in the first three centuries CE it was not because they were Christians *per se*, but because they would not address the emperor properly and honor his divine spirit. This was a serious offense, not just to the emperor, but also to the Roman state. Obeisance was expected as a sign of loyalty to the empire. Thus, when Christians refused to accord the ruler divine respect, they were treated as seditionists.

Tiberius succeeded Octavian and probably was the first ruler to be called "Emperor." He was in power when Jesus died. He ruled 14-37 CE.

Domitian held the office of Emperor from 81-96 CE. It is probable that he was the one who gave the status of "illegal" to Christianity, although the record is not clear whether he issued a firm ruling to that effect. Domitian appears to have authorized prosecution of Christians at least in some parts of the Empire.

From the reign of Trajan (98-117) correspondence survives between him and a subordinate named Pliny. Pliny asked the Emperor for guidance in prosecuting Christians. Trajan replied that as long as Christians did not cause public disturbance or commit criminal acts, they need not be tracked down and prosecuted. Some attempt to limit Christianity was made by Emperor Marcus Aurelius (161-180), and more concerted attempts were made by Emperor Decius (249-251) and Diocletian (284-305). The status of illegality was not removed from Christianity until the late fourth century.

Population Figures

Population figures in the Roman Empire in the time of Jesus have been estimated from the highs for the city of Rome at one million, total population in the Empire from fifty-four to sixty million, Jerusalem at a quarter million, and all Israel at one and a half million; to the lows of half of the above figures. It would seem that the higher figures for Rome and the Empire might be more nearly accurate, but the lower figures for the Jewish areas might be more nearly accurate. Jerusalem's high population estimate may have been skewed by the thousands of pilgrims who came there for the festivals.

It is notable that not all the people who lived in the Jewish lands were Jews. Judea was mostly Jewish, but Galilee probably had as many Gentiles as Jews. Samaria was of Jewish heritage, but had been settled by a predominance of

Assyrians and others over the centuries. Perea probably had more Gentiles than Jews. Moreover, many Jews lived in other countries. The total number of Jews in the Mediterranean world at the time of Jesus has been estimated at a high of five million, and at a low of about half that number.

Those Jews who lived outside of the homeland, the "Diaspora," usually were not so intent on having national sovereignty as those who lived inside the homeland. The Diaspora Jews no doubt would have been proud to have had an autonomous homeland, but generally they were content to participate in the communities where they lived.

In the homeland, however, the political dominance of Rome was a constant irritant in the era of our study of biblical religion. Rome demanded allegiance. Rome required daily sacrifices of animals as a show of allegiance to the state. Rome demanded the payment of taxes from the Jews. Rome demanded peace among all peoples and reacted with immediate, harsh, and sometimes deadly measures to keep the peace.

How oppressive the Roman rule was to Israel during the lifetime of Jesus is open to discussion. Usually there were very few Roman soldiers in Jerusalem or on the streets. The soldiers were stationed on the frontiers of countries in order to ward off invaders. Only at festival times were the troops brought into Jerusalem in order to keep the peace—the Jews had been known to be a bit raucous at festivals, especially at Passover. The Roman official over Jerusalem in 29/30 CE was entitled "prefect"; he usually stayed at a palace in Caesarea, which meant that he was not a constant irritant in Jerusalem. The Roman official over the prefect was the governor stationed in Syria; next in line of command was the emperor.

The official at each level had the authority to do whatever was necessary to keep the peace and secure the empire. Sometimes the prefect in Jerusalem used harsh measures to do so, but in reviewing the history of Israel the prefects may not have been any harsher than Israel's own rulers. In fact, Rome made special concessions to the Jews, such as not having to serve in the armed forces, not displaying Roman standards in Jerusalem, and sometimes winking at the requirement of animal sacrifices to Rome and addressing the emperor as "lord." There is no record that it winked at taxation, however.

It appears that the main complaint of the Jews toward the Roman rule arose from the Covenants between them and God. God had promised them, so they believed, a homeland and nationhood. Rule by Romans, or by any other foreign power, was not what they believed was promised. The Jewish complaint could be lifted only if any and all foreign rulers exited.

Summary

The political background in the Mediterranean world at the time of the birth of Jesus was Roman. Roman rule had many positive features, such as constitutional law, public works and great roads, maritime trade and travel that were quite safe, and a penchant for peace. Christianity would utilize all of these in years to come. Christianity also, after its first century, would be swayed in its own organizational pattern by the imperial structure of Rome. Christianity, however, would find the Roman idea of divinely ordained rule an increasing and sometimes deadly irritant.

It should be noted that the Roman rule over the Jewish homeland aroused great resentment. While resentment usually was present in any country which was dominated by a foreign power, the resentment in Israel was especially relevant to Christianity. The heavy-handed enforcement of *Pax Romana*, the burdensome taxation, the cruel treatment of adversaries, and the violation or ignoring of Jewish laws issued in a mood of despair: humans (Jews) could not remedy this great national misfortune, therefore God needed to act. Ingrained in Jewish thought was that when times were tough, God acted through a messiah to establish righteousness; and if a Kingdom of Heaven could not be established on this Earth, then at least God would establish a Kingdom not of this world.

The Roman political factor has been evaluated by historians as notably hard, cold, and parochial. The Greeks were at hand to provide a more congenial and universal dimension of culture to the Mediterranean world.

Chapter 2

Backgrounds—Greek

Introduction

The dominant cultural background at the time of the birth of Jesus was Greek. While Rome controlled the governmental empire, it made heavy use of Greek social and intellectual bequests to shape its culture. The Greeks elevated social practices and intellectual pursuits to amazing heights. There were many notable Greeks and notable Greek ways that influenced the life-style of the entire Mediterranean world and the beginning years of Christianity. We note a few that are especially relevant to biblical religion.

Early Greek

The Greek factor began with the "Father of Philosophy," Thales (c. 640-546). About the year 600 BCE he began formulating particular truths into universal truth. He was the first person on record to do this logically and systematically. He observed the practical workings of the world around him and then abstracted principles from them. He sought principles more firmly grounded in natural events than in the mystical revelations of such persons as Homer and Hesiod. For example, he could observe that olive trees were individually different, but had enough likeness to be called olive trees rather than, say, cedar trees. This kind of thinking led him to further abstraction, such as there must be a final likeness in all kinds of trees in order for them to be called tree; then to the further conclusion that there must be a final likeness in all things in the entire universe. He had some difficulty selecting a proper term for the ultimate essence.

Finally he chose to denominate it "water," and then merely "stuff."

Thales was a pioneer in that he began this type of philosophical thought with no research materials available—no libraries, textbooks, dictionaries, encyclopedias, internet, or databases. Very soon other Greeks followed in his steps, Greeks such as Anaximenes, Anaximander, Leucippus, and Democritus. One Greek named Heraclitus (c. 536-470) concluded that thought itself was the final abstraction of existence. The word he used was "logos," which fit nicely with Hebrew accounts of creation wherein God thought of something or other, then commanded it to be so, and it emerged. The word "logos" gained further religious significance with the Christian account of beginnings in the first chapter of The Gospel According to John: "In the beginning was the word...." The word "word" in the Gospel is the same in the Greek as "logos." (The Gospel According to John was written in Greek.)

Another cultural notable in the Greek background of Christianity was Pythagoras (c. 572-497) who concentrated on numbers. He viewed numbers as a higher "stuff" than any material element. A number, he noted, could not be contained in a thing. Pythagoras could see two olive trees, but he couldn't see a "two." Two, or any number, was beyond things, hence was more real than things; it was independent and precedent to things. Today we would speak of a "two" as being abstract or metaphysical. Such metaphysical thought would be congenial to Christian conceptions of divinity and spiritual realities.

Another molder of philosophical thought was Parmenides (c. 515-?). He tried to think his way through the puzzle of change and permanence. How, for example could a colt, maybe named "Frisky," be the same Frisky when he grew from a colt to a horse? Was Frisky the adult the same entity as had been Frisky the colt? If no, then there is no problem; but this answer would force the renaming of the original Frisky every time Parmenides saw him because Frisky would be different, even if only slightly, from the time before. If yes, then change had come out of nowhere to add to Frisky's height, weight, and appearance: from where could such material come in order to change Frisky? out of thin air? out of nothing? "Preposterous!" was Parmenides' response. Something cannot be made from nothing. Something has to be made from something; therefore, something always must have existed. When Frisky got old and died he could not be disintegrated into nothing, because something can't become nothing, can't be annihilated. Parmenides tried to solve an extremely difficult problem, one that was not treated by biblical writers, but which became suggestive in the Christian use of the concept of "eternal."

A complication to this problem of change and permanence was given by the aforementioned Heraclitus, who claimed that the only thing permanent in the universe was impermanence. All things change, he declared, just like a flowing river. Other illustrious Greeks tried to bolster Parmenides in opposition to Heraclitus. One of Parmenides' supporters was Zeno of Elea (c. 490-430), known for his "paradoxes." One of Zeno's most famous paradoxes is known as "Achilles and the Tortoise." It describes a race in which the speedy Achilles can never catch the slow Tortoise because of the Parmenidean factor of there always being a half-way point between them. This concentration on the essential nature of the cosmos would be useful to Christian theologians grappling with the essential nature of Jesus.

Two other Greeks of strikingly original thinking were Leucippus (fl. 450-420) and Democritus (c. 460-370). They contemplated the "stuff" of the universe and theorized that it was the "atom," a smallest unit of matter which could not be cut smaller. Their theory held true for two thousand years until the atom was cut/split, but the principle remained true beyond the cut/split that there is an essential something, or energy, or string that is final and cannot be divided further. Their work broached the question of basic reality in the universe, whether it was spirit or matter or divinity or love or what, a question early Christians would similarly debate.

Another Greek philosopher, Diogenes (c. 400-325), was the multi-faceted character called the "Cynic." Among his talents was that of being a moral evangelist. He traveled from place to place proclaiming ethical truths and urging people to be good. He believed that every person has a spark of the divine and is called to be true to the fullness from which that spark comes. Diogenes is credited with a form of speaking called the "diatribe," translated into Christian vernacular as "sermon." His talk of a spark of the divine was welcome to a significant variety of Christianity in the first two centuries.

Let us skip other Greeks in order to get to three of the most famous: Socrates, Plato, and Aristotle. Their contributions to culture are so numerous that volumes have been written and still are being written on each of them. From them a few concepts can be singled out that have relationship to biblical religion in our era of study.

Classical Greek

Socrates (c. 470-399) was the oldest of the three. He sought Thales' "stuff" in the realm of virtue. He sought to define the particular virtues and to abstract the highest virtue of the human being. He shied from getting information from divine revelations because they had so many contradictions to common sense. He asserted that the highest virtue of a human is to be fully human; that is, by analogy, an Attican lion can be expected to be fully lion if it develops all the capacities of an Attican lion; just so regarding a human, that a human can be expected to be fully human if it develops all the capacities of a human. The same allegory could apply to a pony, or a porcupine, or a pineapple. If any one of these were meant to be something else—say a pony were meant to be a porcupine—then it would have been created so; and the human likewise. Therefore, the search for what is fully human is the goal. Socrates spent his days in this search, and just after the turn of the fifth century BCE gave his life because he wouldn't recant this search. His pursuit of virtue was a precursor to Jesus' extension of law to intent and inner purity.

Plato (c. 428-348) was Socrates' student. He followed Socrates in his quest. It was he who "wrote" Socrates inasmuch as we have no written works from Socrates. Plato wrote Socrates by making him the principal character in many of his "Dialogues." Plato added to Socratic thought the positing of eternal Forms that inform all matter as to what it will be. For example, there is a Form of a horse before there are any horses; if it were not so, then the hair, hide, mane, et al, would not know whether to be a horse, or a camel, or a rat, or whatever. It would be the same with a Greek theatre: without a Form the blocks of stone would sprawl all over in some kind of amorphous jumble. Plato posited further that there must be a supreme Form beyond all lesser Forms, beyond all classes and particulars. He called this Form the "Good," a term quite in keeping with Socrates' view, and a term which the Christian movement later could shorten to "God."

Aristotle (384-322) was Plato's pupil. He made a number of additions to Plato's work. Aristotle analyzed the process of thinking, that is, the work of logos, so thoroughly that he was able to set down the process in formal logic. He discovered that given knowledge could lead to further knowledge if steps for doing so were followed logically. Two of his concepts that are friendly to Christian thinking are 1)that since every effect has a cause there must be a First Cause, and 2)that since there is motion in the universe there must be a Prime Mover. As you can surmise, First Cause and Prime Mover are very compatible with biblical religion. Then this further point: Aristotle looked for Plato's posited Forms and could find none. He concluded that the Forms, instead of being separate and beyond actual things, were lodged within actual things—something had to be present in order for a something to be a something. Such a view could give assurance to the Christian movement in its claim that the Word (Logos) had been on Earth in the flesh. Additionally, Aristotle's teleology claimed that the potential strove to become actual, which has at least these two implications: the divine has a potential yearning to become actual, and does so when it is incarnated; and the potentiality in humans has a yearning to become actual as the divine is actual. Such thinking would be useful in Christian circles as evidence that God has purpose for history, and that God has the yearning to turn potentiality into actuality. This line of thinking also would be appropriate to the validation of the presence of Jesus in the ritual of the Lord's Supper.

There were later Greek philosophers who could be cited in connection with biblical religion, especially Epicurus (341-270) who counseled a life of moderation and distancing oneself from public affairs. Also Zeno of Citium (c. 334-262) who advised persons to follow the natural order of life and to do so without complaint about what happens, whether a person is a king or a slave. Zeno's "keep your chin up no matter what happens to you" attitude toward life was labeled "Stoicism." Epicurus' and Zeno's claims would show in aspects of the life-style of many early Christians.

Hellenistic Greek

In the fourth century BCE, during the last years of Aristotle's life, a young man from Macedonia conquered Greece and much of the rest of the world all the way to India. He was Alexander, called "The Great." His greatness lay partially in his military prowess. More important to our study was his greatness in cultural affairs. He attempted to remold the whole of society by a plan that came to be called "Hellenism." In brief, he attempted to establish a world-wide culture by sifting from the civilizations he conquered what he thought were the best features. He had been tutored by Aristotle to value what was finest for the body, mind, and soul.

Alexander built new cities and repopulated old cities with mixtures of peoples who were expected to embrace those features. Just in the region of Israel, he built ten cities called the "Decapolis" on the other side of the Jordan River and the

Sea of Galilee. The Decapolis was featured in an incident in Jesus' ministry when he sent the evil spirits from the Gadarene demoniac into a herd of pigs which rushed down a hillside into the Sea of Galilee and were drowned; the Hellenistic herdsmen were mightily upset about their loss of livestock. This technique of mixing peoples and values had economic benefits, too, and served Alexander's strategic goal of establishing a world culture for his world rule.

The full implementation of Hellenism was dealt a blow by the early death of Alexander at the age of thirty-three in 323 BCE. His rule was a mere thirteen years, 336-323. He had no adequate heirs to succeed him. Consequently his empire was split among his four leading generals. For the most part they supported and promoted Hellenism, but without Alexander's genius or charisma. The Romans generally were open to and adopted much of Hellenism.

The Jews were another story. They generally rejected Hellenism, mainly for theological reasons. They clung to their own laws, festivals, and customs. The younger Jews were open to some of the Greek ways in order to be *avante-garde*: there are accounts of Jewish young men who joined a Hellenistic type of health club, called the "Gym(nasium)" much to the displeasure and severe punishment of their fathers. Even the fathers, however, were touched by Hellenism a couple centuries before Jesus when they welcomed the translation of the Jewish/Hebrew scriptures into the *lingua franca*, Greek; that translation was called the "Septuagint," or "LXX" ("Seventy") for short, and is still a highly respected work. The resettlement of peoples and the aspect of ecumenicity would be aids to the Christian movement.

Alexander's generals who began the dynasties that most affected biblical religion were in Egypt and Syria. These two regimes were intent on subduing one another. The land between them included Israel. As the fortunes of the two dynasties waxed and waned, first one, then the other ruled Israel. In 168 BCE the Syrian Seleucid dynasty, which was ruled by Antiochus Epiphanes IV held power over Israel. He pushed Hellenism so forcefully and undiplomatically on the Jews that the Jewish Hasmonean family led a rebellion against Syria, and won. The Hasmoneans were hailed with messianic plaudits. They brought freedom once again to Israel. The people commemorated the event by instituting the Chanukkah festival in 165 BCE. This freedom lasted for about a hundred years before the Romans annexed Israel and reduced the Hasmoneans to puppets.

The effects of Hellenism on Jewish life were varied. The old line Jews resisted every bit of Hellenism. The younger generation vacillated before it. The Jewish provinces of Galilee and Perea, populated by as many or more Gentiles than Jews, were more open to it than the provinces of Samaria and Judea. The Jews in the Diaspora, those who lived in places outside of Israel, were most open to Hellenism. Regardless of the degree of openness, it probably is safe to say that all practicing Jews were anti-Hellenistic in some measure and hoped for a messianic intrusion by YHWH to establish the ideal universal culture, or at least a Kingdom of God in Israel, a hope very much in evidence in early Christian circles.

In spite of Jewish opposition, Hellenism had these additional benefits which would be factors in the spread of the Christian movement. Hellenism emphasized education. It made provision for every free boy to receive extensive education, and may have made the first provision anywhere for free girls to receive at least basic education. Christianity largely would be perpetuated by the educated.

Hellenism also used the Greek language. It became the commercial language of the Mediterranean world and continued to be so for centuries. While Jesus and his disciples spoke the local dialect of Aramaic, all of the New Testament was written in Greek. The language itself was word-rich: it had appropriate words so that precise meanings could be given to each word, in contrast to our English which can have ten or twenty meanings to a single word. To this day Christian scholars study Hellenistic/Koine Greek in order to extract the exact meanings of the New Testament writings.

Hellenism also promoted athletic games. Not only the workouts in the gymnasia but also the many public games at many levels brought together persons of all nationalities and cultures, similar to what our present day Olympics do. A notable difference between the games then and now is that the Greek games generally were friendlier than our current nationalistic-oriented Olympics. Their games valued individual performance measured in time, distance, or endurance, rather than in the quantity of medals this or that national team wins. Mixing of people would be a characteristic of the Christian church.

Greek Religion

Hellenism probably did not originate any religions intentionally, but it did encourage religious devotion. It honored the traditional gods of Greece. It respected their temples that still are acclaimed as some of the world's finest architecture. It made provision for the celebration of numerous festivals to honor the gods. It was culturally proper for the Greeks to include the aura of religious devotion in their life-style. This aura of religious devotion would be helpful to the evangelists of early Christianity.

An additional facet of the culture involved another type of religion, the Mystery religions. The beliefs and practices of the dozen or so Mystery religions prefigured several features of Christianity. One feature was that each of them claimed to have a special revelation from the divinity in regard to human duty and destiny.

Another feature of the Mystery religions was that they formed supportive fellowships for their members. They provided a sense of community in the midst of the multinational world of Hellenism. One of Hellenism's concomitant banes was that while it fostered a one-world ambience, it also uprooted persons from pasts that may have been more secure.

Also, the Mystery religions developed a number of sacraments for its members. There were rituals for initiation into and continued participation in the religions. One initiation rite was a type of baptism by sprinkling initiates with blood or wine. An ongoing rite was a type of communion in which food and drink, either consecrated to or representative of the divinity, were taken ceremonially. The emblems were equivalent to ingesting the divinity in order that the partaker might be transformed into the likeness of the divinity. In America we are familiar with the ritual of Indians partaking of a totem animal in order to take on the strengths of that animal. In the Mystery religions the union of a person with the divine or the divine quality, was called "apotheosis," which could take place in the present and carry on into eternity. If one were a faithful participant one could be beatified and/or deified. The sacraments were observed in closed fellowship meetings.

Also, Mystery religion mythology contended that this world was less than good, that the divine world was wholly good; therefore, as a person lessened relationship with this world and cultivated relationship with the divine world, estrangement between humanity and divinity would be remedied. Persons began the remedying by confessing their sins and/or ignorance of their truly intended destiny of unity with divinity, and then proceeded with observance of the rituals and various regulations.

Probably the largest of the Mystery religions was that of Isis. Two others were very popular, Cybele and Dionysus. Still another, Mystra, was so widespread and so akin to the Christian movement that for awhile in the second and third centuries CE it threatened to overwhelm Christianity. Illustrative of the popularity of the Mystery religions was the number of temples in the city of Pompeii, a resort city near Rome that was buried by a volcano in 79 CE. Archeologists have discovered over forty major temples of various Mystery religions in this city which had approximately twenty-five thousand residents—a huge number of temples for a city that size, even taking into account the tourist trade.

One big difference between Hellenistic or Roman, and Jewish or Christian religions was the number of gods who could be worshipped. For the former, many gods could be worshipped; the gods were not jealous. For the latter, only one God could be worshipped; God was jealous. This difference would be important in early Christianity when allegiance to the divine spirit of the emperor was required: the Christians were accused of being atheists because they would not worship the traditional Greek/Roman gods in addition to their own singular divinity.

Summary

The cultural dimension in the Mediterranean world at the time of the birth of Jesus was Greek. The culture was denominated, "Hellenism." It was the creation of Alexander the Great who remolded the Western world all the way to India. After Alexander's death his successors continued the promotion of Hellenism. In time Rome conquered the successors, but it kept many aspects of Hellenism intact. Many aspects of Greek culture found a home in Christianity.

Beyond the Roman Rule and the Greek culture, Jewish religion furnished a further background setting for Christianity.

Chapter 3

Backgrounds—Jewish

Introduction

The religious dimension in the background of the Christian movement was primarily Jewish. Both Roman rule and Greek culture were significant factors in the history of Christianity, and they did include some religion aspects. The Jews, however, contributed seminal religion concepts: basic religion tradition, canon of sacred scripture, customs, rituals, theology, religion Parties, institutions, and literature.

Basic Religion Tradition

The basic religion tradition could be stated in terms of Covenants. The Abrahamic Covenant carried the tradition of a chosen people who by God's power would become a great nation and a blessing to all nations. This Covenant was general, perhaps more like a handshake than a legal document.

The Mosaic Covenant which followed was a legal agreement wherein God set the commandments and laws and the people pledged conformity. The most famous part of this Covenant is the Ten Commandments. Over the years about six hundred other commandments were added which covered nearly every type of behavior, including diet. This Covenant carried with it a retributive condition, that human obedience brought blessing from God, while disobedience brought misfortune. This Covenant was meant to be a joyous guide for behavior rather than a burdensome task. Its core was summed up as love of God and love of neighbor.

The Davidic Covenant which followed the Mosaic was a dynastic one that legitimized the rule of David's family over Israel forever. It was based on the belief that if God directly used the monarch as the builder of the nation and the director of righteousness—as a messiah—then the chosen people would find fulfillment and would reflect the image of God in and for the world.

These were the formal Covenants. Another type of Covenant was advocated by the prophets, notably Jeremiah. He claimed that the best Covenant of all involved the heart. In his famous characterization in chapter 31 of the book by his name, he proclaimed that the best, the most transforming, the most redeeming, the most God-pleasing of all covenantal relationships between God and humans was the inward attitude which eschewed all pretenses and prides and longed only for a passionate attachment to God. It was a Covenant to be made by each individual quite apart from whatever the nation might do.

Canon of Sacred Scripture

In addition to Covenants, the Jewish canon of sacred scripture was of great significance to the Christian movement. Jesus was a Jew who revered the scriptures. The Apostles were Jews who revered the scriptures. The writers of the Gospels revered the scriptures. The missionary Paul revered the scriptures. Indeed, the leaders of the first four centuries of Jesus followers revered the Jewish scriptures so much that they attached them to the Christian writings and called them the "Old Testament." There was no commonly accepted "New Testament" until near the end of the fourth century.

Jesus used the scriptures as the basis of his teaching. He sometimes enriched them with further insights into their meanings. He cited them to legitimize his own calling and ministry. He quoted them when it came to a succinct summation of the human-divine relationship.

The Jewish scriptures were revered not because they were the only ones available. There were other sacred books in the first century world. There was the mythology of Mesopotamia. There was the Egyptian Book of the Dead. There were the works of Homer and Hesiod, revered by some as holy books. There were the books of the Mystery religions, books of other national, regional, and local religions. There was no dearth of sacred books; but the ones that became normative for Christian use were those of Jewish origination.

Customs, Rituals, and Theology

The customs, rituals, and theology of Jewish religion greatly influenced beginning Christianity. The customary mark of Jewishness was circumcision for the males. Paul led the Christian movement in dropping the requirement of circumcision for membership in the church, but many continued and/or advocated circumcision anyway.

The custom of giving a tithe of one's income to religious causes was continued.

The custom of worshippers meeting in congregation carried over from synagogue to church.

The ritual of sacrifice of the unblemished to God was carried through in the characterization of Jesus as the sacrificial lamb (although Jewish theology did not consider the lamb to be a means of atonement for sin; the lamb theme was introduced in The Gospel According to John).

The ritual festival of Pesach/Passover and its accompanying sacred meal were modified into the Lord's Supper.

The rituals of repentance and baptism were continued as signs of commitment to God. Forms of these became standard among Christians (although it should be noted that the Mystery religions also furnished types of these for Christianity).

The dominant feature of the Jewish background for the Christian movement was theology. God, variously designated as "El," "Elohim," or "YHWH"/"Yahweh," or "Adonai," or "Lord," was believed to be the one and only living God. God was eternal. God was the creator of all that is. God was the director of history. God was the fateful force for all humanity. God was the source of wisdom. God was the just, merciful, shepherding, and serving divinity all at once. God expected obedience to his will, but offered forgiveness to those who fell short. God healed. God redeemed. God saved. God gave a good creation to humans so that they could be fruitful and multiply.

God was believed to be a personal deity who could speak, see, hear, and smell (no record of touch; the post-resurrection Jesus told Mary not to touch him). God was believed to have human-like emotions in that God could love, be offended, be repentant, be merciful, and had human welfare at heart. On the other hand, God was believed to be transcendent, beyond human frailties, so awesome that not even God's name should be uttered. From the Hebrews to the Jews to the Christians the belief was that God was fully in charge of all that exists, and together they could say, "God is God."

Religion Parties

Another part of the Jewish heritage was the "Parties" or varieties within the religion. These are mentioned in Christian literature, but a caution flag is that the Christian literature was penned decades after Jesus, so that its usually derogatory portrayal of these Parties may reflect later conflicts with them.

In Jesus' time, one of the Parties was the Pharisees. They were "separated ones" dedicated to living the most righteous lives possible. They usually avoided traffic with the established economic and political factions. The Pharisees probably originated several decades before Jesus as a protest movement to Hellenism.

While the Pharisees were strict disciplinarians as far as religious practice went, they were on the cutting edge of theology. They believed that the Law of Moses ought to be adapted to contemporary needs; hence they perpetuated the oral tradition of the Law. They personalized the relationship with God and called God "Father." They developed demonology and angelology. They led simple lives, sought conversion of the heart, and promoted love and justice as the ways of true religion. They promoted the use of the synagogue. This Party drew allegiance from all classes of the

Jews, primarily from those without great wealth or power, although there are mentions of a few priests and scribes being members. Only a very few Pharisees are mentioned as being members of the Sanhedrin, the ruling council of the Jews.

The Pharisees probably were quite in tune with Jesus in his day. The vehement attacks on them as found in the Gospels seem out of place. Since the Gospels were written decades after Jesus death, it may be that they reflect the general animosity that grew up between the Jews and the Christians about 68 CE and following, rather than an animosity during Jesus' time. Certainly the Pharisees could have differed from Jesus on some points of the Law, but then any two Jews of any Party could have done the same. The historian Josephus gives an estimate of core membership in the Pharisees as six thousand about the year 70 CE. They became the tradition bearers of the Jewish religion after the destruction of Jerusalem and the Temple.

Another Party was the Sadducees. The name of this Party probably was derived from "zadok," or "saddouk," meaning "righteous." The Sadducees became prominent during the reign of the Hasmonean, John Hyrcanus (134-104). The Sadducees were the aristocratic class who maintained their wealth and influence by collaborating with the regime in power. By the time of Jesus the Sadducees also controlled the high priesthood and Temple. They were more conservative, even reactionary, in comparison to the Pharisees. They accepted only the Law as written in the five books of Moses, and they interpreted them literally. They denied the cutting edge theology common to the Pharisees and Jesus; especially they rejected the concepts of resurrection and afterlife. They were fewer in number than the Pharisees. They disappeared after the Jewish-Roman War.

A third Party in Jewish life was the Zealots. While the New Testament mentions the Zealots, there is doubt by some scholars that the Zealots had come into existence by the time of Jesus. At least the Zealots were in existence at the start of the Jewish-Roman War in 66 CE. Since the Gospels appear to have been written after this date, the authors might have assumed that the Zealots existed all along. Whether or not the Party existed in Jesus' day, their sentiment did. The Zealots opposed any foreign rule. They were willing to give their lives as patriots in order to rid Israel of occupation. One highly dedicated cadre within the Zealots was called the "Sicarii," the "knife-men." They vowed to trade their lives, one on one, if they could kill a Roman soldier. In addition they slew fellow Jews seen as cooperating with Rome. They killed by the use of a small, curved dagger which they hid up the sleeves of their cloaks. The Zealots were zealous not only for national autocracy, but also for YHWH. They buttressed their dedication with a firm faith that God would empower them to overcome any and all opposition. They acted on this faith by starting the Jewish-Roman War in 66 CE, but they were annihilated by the Romans.

A fourth Party was the Essenes. They were known as the "Hasayya," or "Pious Ones." They were similar to the Pharisees, but went even further in separating themselves from the unclean world around them. They considered both the Romans and their fellow Jews as having been corrupted by the world. They probably were the ones who began communes in the desert, and may have been the ones who hid copies of the scriptures now known as the Dead Sea Scrolls.

The Essenes claimed that God had given them secret information that enabled them to know the correct interpretation of the Law. They constructed large baptistries for their initiation rite. They instituted a sacred meal of bread and wine. They preached a new covenant and a new age. They preferred the biblical books of Deuteronomy, Psalms, and Isaiah, the same three most-quoted books in the Christian New Testament. They maintained a very strict ascetic type social code and a hierarchical structure.

There were two drawbacks to the Essenes being widespread. The first was their life-style. They observed celibacy, exclusion of handicapped persons, and avoidance of any contact with those they considered unclean. They required a three year trial period before accepting a person as a member, and they had strict rules of behavior which, if violated, could result in immediate dismissal. They shared their possessions, read the scriptures continually, and anticipated persecution from outside religious and/or political authorities. They expected the soon coming of a great "Teacher of Righteousness," who either would be the messianic person or the herald of the messianic age. The estimates of their numbers during the time of Jesus range from a thousand to four thousand.

The second drawback to Essenes being widespread was that they apparently defied the Romans at the close of the Jewish-Roman War and were annihilated.

Lesser Parties or types of Parties are mentioned. The Herodians may not have been an official Party; they were supporters of the Herodian dynasty. The Scribes were more of a fraternity of attorneys who knew and interpreted the Law, who matched legal wits with Jesus from time to time, and who are accused in the Gospels of persecuting the Jesus Followers after the crucifixion. The Samaritans lived in the province of Samaria and thought that the inhabitants of the other provinces were despicable; they did expect a messiah of prophetic character to arrive soon. The Chief Priests are not specifically identified, but probably were an informal or luncheon group of current and past high priests.

In addition to the Parties and types of Parties there were the Am Ha-ares, the "people of the land." These were the common people, peasants, of Israel who constituted the bulk of the population. They observed those portions of the Law that suited them. They were not considered reliable witnesses in court. They were the favorites of Jesus—the ones who were as "sheep without a shepherd."

Institutions

Also of importance in the Jewish background to Christianity were certain institutions of Jewish faith and life. The Temple was one. The Temple was the center piece of the Hebrew/Jewish saga. It was the only place that sacrifices could be made. Its priests conducted the finest rituals and presented the greatest music. It housed the very dwelling place of God. It was a magnificent structure. Its courtyard was twenty-six acres in size. It attracted tourists as well as worshippers.

The Temple was in the charge of the high priest who alone could enter the holy of holies where the very presence of God dwelt. He could enter only once a year for the ritual of atonement. The Temple was served by twenty-four groups of priests who rotated sacrificial duties throughout the year. It was served further by a special group of priests called "Levites" who were the functionaries for services such as music, policing, and custodial care. The workers were supported by the half-shekel tax, various offerings, and a portion of the sacrifices.

At the Temple, offerings and sacrifices were made twice daily, at nine in the morning and three in the afternoon. The populace gathered at those times to watch and pray. When the Romans annexed Jerusalem they added their own offering and sacrifice requirements: twice daily offerings of two lambs and an ox as symbols of allegiance to Rome; these were hated symbols to the Jews.

The Temple in Jesus' time was the second one built on that site. The first one, attributed to King Solomon, was destroyed in a war with the Babylonians in 587/586 BCE. It was rebuilt about seventy years later, but it was such a pitiful replica that Herod the Great finally authorized the remodeling of the second Temple to meet, even exceed, the beauty of the original Temple. This remodeling stretched over three-quarters of a century and was finished just a few years before the Jewish-Roman War 66-70 CE. The story is told that in the War the Roman general, Titus, gave orders not to destroy this magnificent structure; but when his soldiers broke into Jerusalem in a final assault—having chaffed for months at merely camping outside the walls to maintain a siege—they were in no mood to spare anything. Against orders they threw firebrands into the Temple. The building was destroyed completely and has never been rebuilt. Probably it never will be rebuilt inasmuch as an extraordinary Muslim mosque, the Dome of the Rock, has stood on the site for centuries.

The Temple had aspects such as office and music that were influential on beginning Christianity, but perhaps the most influential was the mood. The Temple inspired respect for things holy and awe for YHWH/God. Also, Christians used the figure of the Temple in their writings.

A second institution was the synagogue. This was a fellowship/meeting house for the purposes of study and prayer. It arose because of the Babylonian victory over the Jews in the sixth century BCE. Since the Jews had no place to meet after the Babylonians destroyed the first Temple, and since the leading religious Jews were exiled to Babylon, the synagogue was invented by the religion leaders in Babylon as the vehicle for the continuation of the faith. It was a popular institution: only ten men of age, a "minyan," were required to form a synagogue. A synagogue at first was the gathering of the members; later the term also was applied to the building in which they met. The group gathered for "beth din," judgment and discipline; for "beth midrash," education; for "beth tefillah," prayer; and for "beth kenesseth," meetings.

The synagogues continued as local means to express devotion to God even after the Temple was rebuilt. In the synagogue any Jewish male of age could read the scriptures, make comments, or lead the prayers, whereas in the Temple the priesthood performed all the ministries. In addition, the synagogue differed from the Temple in that each synagogue elected its own ruler; if the synagogue were in a Hellenistic environment the synagogue could include women and a woman could be a ruler.

In time, synagogue buildings were constructed. They usually were rectangular in shape with the front oriented toward Jerusalem. Each synagogue had a platform, "bema," with a reading stand; a candle stand, "menorah"; and a chief seat. Behind these in a niche in the wall was the repository—"ark"—for the scrolls of the sacred scriptures. Usually there were benches along the walls. There might be guest rooms for travelers and dignitaries attached to the outer walls.

Literature

The sacred literature of the Jews was a special bequest to the Christian movement. The most revered body of sacred literature was the Bible. It contained twenty-four books (it contains the same text as the Christian Old Testament, but is arranged in a different manner). It was written in Hebrew, although there is some opinion that a few of the latest works were written in part or in whole in Aramaic. It was translated prior to the Christian movement into the Greek language and was called the Septuagint/LXX. (The Bible also is designated in our time by the term "Tenakh," which is an acrostic of the first few letters of each of the divisions: Law—Torah, Prophets—Nevi-im, and Writings—Kethubim.) The most important division was the Law, especially as recorded in the Pentateuch/Five Books of Moses, the first five books of the Bible—Genesis, Exodus, Leviticus, Numbers, and Deuteronomy.

When the written Law was not specific enough to cover a given situation, the scholars set forth interpretations. For example, the Law stated that an "unblemished" animal was to be sacrificed; but how unblemished should unblemished be? especially since hardly any animal was totally free of imperfections or of multi-colored hair. Consequently the scholars discussed and debated an answer. Their comments were not put into the Bible, but were transmitted orally at first, then in writing later. At some point a few hundred years before Jesus, the scribes began writing down the comments. This Oral Law was very important to a Party such as the Pharisees, but not so important to a Party such as the Sadducees. Jesus developed the Law in an Oral Law manner: he kept the Law, but added to its original meanings.

As the years passed the Oral Law was collected into a "Mishnah" volume—actually two Mishnahs, one originating in Babylon and one originating in Jerusalem. Even the Mishnahs sometimes did not give a final word of Law, so commentaries on the Mishnahs called "Midrashim" were composed. Over the centuries most of this material outside of the Bible has been collected into a many-volume work called the "Talmud." The Christians who had a Jewish background were familiar with the Oral Law, but the Gentile converts generally had scant knowledge of it. In time the Christians began writing their own oral law in the form of commentaries on the books of the New Testament.

Another piece of Jewish literature highly respected in the desert community at Qumran, and possibly among the Essenes, was the Manual of Discipline. It gave the rationale for withdrawal from the world, and it gave detailed directions for the life and order of the desert communities. There is a legend that John the Baptist was an Essene, and the manner and teaching of Jesus are so similar to the material in the Manual that some think he must have spent time with the Essenes. The Manual may have been used by Christians at the first, but finally was dropped from use.

Other Jewish literatures that were widely read but which did not achieve New Testament standing among Christians have been lumped together under the nomer of Deuterocanon. According to which scholar is giving an opinion, the Deuterocanon can include the Apocrypha, the Peudepigrapha, and sometimes other works. These literatures were produced about the time of the production of the Septuagint, or later, and did not have time to gain enough support to be included in the most sacred body of scripture, the Bible. These books contain chronicles, poetry, wisdom literature, apocalyptic material, and religious fiction. In general they hope for a better world, a coming of the Kingdom of God, and the expectation of a messianic savior to reestablish national freedom for the Jews. Many of these works have been placed in versions of the Christian Bible in a special section between the Old and New Testaments.

One Jewish philosopher whose works were never given anything like a canonical status, but have been influential in the development of Christian doctrine was Philo (30 BCE—50 CE). He was a Jew of the Diaspora who lived in Alexandria. He attempted to combine Jewish theology with

Greek philosophy. He claimed that Moses talked about the same things that the philosophers discussed, but in allegorical language. He claimed that Socrates, Plato, and Aristotle drew their ideas from the Bible. He exhorted the Jews to think in universal terms. He put a capital "L" on the Greek term "logos," and designated it as the creative agent through whom the transcendent God worked in the world. Philo's books were used by Christian writers in the early centuries of the Christian movement.

Another Jewish author who provided information about the life and times in Israel during and just after the lifetime of Jesus was Joseph ben Matthias, popularly known by the Roman name Flavius Josephus (c. 37-100). He was a Jew who had command of troops in Galilee at the beginning of the Jewish-Roman War in 66 CE. He defected to the Romans, was given asylum, and wrote histories of the Jews and of the times.

Summary

The religion dimension in the land where Jesus lived and where Christianity began was Jewish. It furnished a foundation for Christianity. It bequeathed a canon of sacred scripture that was the only sacred scripture for Christianity at the beginning. Its customs and rituals had many facets that were adopted and adapted by Christianity. Its theology was accepted almost wholly by Christianity. Its religion Parties and institutions supplied prototypes for Christian order. Its extensive literature gave large measures of substance and form to Christianity.

Christianity was very much a child of Jewish religion, although an increasingly rebellious child as the years passed.

With these Roman, Greek, and Jewish backgrounds in place, the stage is set for our consideration of the central figure of Christianity, Jesus.

Part II

Jesus

Chapter 4

Jesus—Sources

Focus on Jesus

The impetus for the Christian movement was Jesus. He must have been one very outstanding individual. Countless volumes have been written about him, but none has established beyond a doubt what his uniqueness was. Early on he was described as the fellow who lived down the street, the son of Joseph and Mary. Later he was described as the divine son of God. It would be a boon to our study if we had Jesus' diary; instead we only know that he wrote a few words in the sand. It would be helpful to have material about his Earthly life that was historically timely, from his Twelve Disciples or even from disinterested reporters. Alas we have primarily four Gospels according to four otherwise unknown persons from a later era whose first intent was to give faith-statements rather than historical datum.

Nevertheless, we must do our best to describe the life and work of Jesus. He was the starting point of the Christian Way. He was the focal point of the Twelve Disciples, the apostles, and all of the members of the Way. Even though he and the incredibly successful evangelist, Paul, were not personally acquainted during Jesus' lifetime, Jesus was the reason for the religion and the work of Paul. The succeeding generations of Christians created many creeds both short and long in attempts to describe Jesus. It can be said that without the historical Jesus there would be no historical Christianity.

Principal Sources: The Four Gospels

The Gospels According to Mark, Matthew, Luke, and John are our principal sources for the study of Jesus. There are a few other works which were not included in the New Testament which give information about Jesus. We shall use these, too, although sparingly.

Note carefully that "Gospels" are faith-statements primarily, that is, experience accounts. These are the ways in which the writers perceived Jesus. They are not documents which we would call "histories." Their writers gave to us their versions of the religious meaning of Jesus. It was not so important to these writers that the chronology of events in Jesus' life was accurate or that a physical description of Jesus was drawn. Indeed, it is possible and probable that neither Mark, Matthew, Luke, nor John met the historical Jesus. Add to this the very widespread belief during the first century in the Christian movement that Jesus was resurrected after his crucifixion and was coming again—soon; since Jesus was coming it was not necessary to write "histories"—Jesus would be there in person.

The four New Testament Gospels were written about forty to as much as eighty years after the death of Jesus. As far as we can tell, the first editions had no authors attributed to them. They were anonymous. The names by which we call them now were attached years later. The appellation "The Gospel According to" also was a later addition, evidently a notice to the readers that the Gospels were the faith-statements of particular persons, with the implication that other persons might have different versions. Also note that the Gospels are not entitled, "The Gospel According to Jesus."

Scholarly Study of the Sources

Many, many scholars have devoted lifetimes to the study of Jesus according to these four Gospels. Scholars especially from the nineteenth century forward have examined not only the content but also the technical aspects, aspects such as who were the authors, why did they write, from where did they write, to whom did they write, when did they write, and the like. They have examined the language used, the sources used, the writing style, the editorial notations, and the personal biases of the authors. They have sought to reconstruct the social, psychological, and cultural milieux of the time in which Jesus lived to discern how these affected the writing of the four Gospels. They have studied the Gospels as thoroughly as any other literature in the world.

The intense study of the Gospels in these ways began about 1850 CE. Before this date, the Gospels customarily were read uncritically. Then scholars began taking particular notice of both major and minor differences between the Gospels. These differences caused some consternation. The previous assumption had been for centuries that God personally saw to the transmission if not the actual writing of the scriptures. The scholars awakened to the situation that if God were the direct or indirect source of the Gospels, why were there differences? Was God forgetful of what God said first to this writer and then to the next writer? Did God make mistakes? Before this, the differences had been overlooked or the accounts conflated. For example, when The Gospels According to Matthew and Luke tell about the birth of Jesus, one has the wise men coming and the other has the shepherds coming; most Christmas plays even in our time include both of these comings as happening at the birth of the infant; but a critical study has realized that the wise men could not have come hundreds of miles on camels in a single ride following a star which could pinpoint a singular site and be at the manger on the birth night; and that shepherds did not tend their sheep at night.

This wise men-shepherds item turned out to be one of the minor ones, since it would not materially affect the salvation event of Jesus. As scholars studied the rest of the Gospels they found far more substantial differences in such portions as the genealogy, parentage, teachings, and Passion narratives. At a still deeper level they found differences in opinion of the basic nature of Jesus, ranging from fully human to fully divine. Countless scholars joined the search to get back to the actual Jesus, not to discredit Jesus, but to find out who he was, what he said, and what he did in order to appreciate the real person.

The results of the work of such scholars fill many volumes, readily available in most libraries. Here are three major results of these careful studies.

1. Oral stories.

The first of three major results of scholarly study of the Gospel sources was the realization that behind the Gospels there were oral stories about Jesus. The oral stories would have been older than the written stories, and thus ought to tell more accurately who Jesus was. The oral material probably was told not in chronological order, but in such manner as we tell stories to each other about events gone by, using such words as, "Remember when…"; or "That reminds me of the time…"; and the like. Since the span of time between the death of Jesus and the writing of the first Gospel was about forty years, you can imagine how many stories might have been told. Furthermore, you can imagine how they might have come to differ—this or that detail dropped from memory, and this or that part retaining more meaning for the story teller than some other part. You can imagine how stories would be modified innocently just by being told from one person to the next. This type of study is not done in order to claim that any of the stories in the Gospels are false, but to find out which stories were closest to the original events and hence most authentic.

2. Different sources.

A second major result of scholarly study was the discovery that the Gospel writers used different sources to compose their accounts. The attempt to identify these sources became a prime concern. The attempt involved inquiring about the social, regional, and theological assumptions of the sources. It asked which writers used which sources? Did any two or more of the writers use the same sources? Why did the writers select the materials they actually selected? Source study asked why did the writers leave out great chunks of material considering all that Jesus must have said and done?

One of the discoveries was that a further point had been overlooked for centuries: none of the writers of the

Gospels were present with Jesus, so how could the writers relate word for word conversations between Jesus and others when they weren't even there?

An outcome of this source examination was that three of the Gospels had some identical material, as well as some original material. The fourth Gospel was different in many, many ways. Therefore, the three were given a nickname of the "Synoptic Gospels," which meant that they saw many things with the same eye.

Analysis of the three Gospels indicated that Mark was the first to be written. Great portions of Mark are cited by Matthew and Luke—about six hundred of the six hundred sixty-one verses in Mark are repeated in Matthew or Luke, or in both Matthew and Luke. This indicates the "priority of Mark." In addition, Matthew and Luke had material which Mark didn't have. Moreover, Matthew had some material that Luke didn't have, and visa versa. These factors meant that there was a Mark source, a Matthew-Luke source designated by scholars as "Q" (German for "Quelle," "writing"), a Matthew source, and a Luke source. Source study is an attempt to get back to the oldest, presumably most authentic accounts of the Jesus event.

3. Editing/redacting.

A third major result of scholarly study was the discovery that the very composition of the Gospels involved editing (often called "redacting") the materials at hand. Obviously the writers used or didn't use some of the materials, shortened or lengthened some of the materials, and explained in extended language or parenthetical remarks what they thought their particular readers might not understand. Furthermore, scholars tried to discern what editorial remarks were mandated by the lapse of time between the death of Jesus about 29/30 CE and the writing of the Gospels about forty to as much as eighty years later. Surely the social, political, economic, and cultural scenes changed over that many years. What were the Gospel writers trying to tell the readers in these subsequent ages? What does each of the Gospels as a whole tell about their own attributed authors?

An example of this kind of careful redaction study can be seen in The Gospel According to Mark. At the time Jesus lived, Mark probably was a very young child, or if he had an average lifespan for that era of about forty years, he might not have been born when Jesus died. When would Mark have become interested in the Jesus event? Let's be generous and say age fifteen. How did he know anything about Jesus? He heard the older generation telling stories and giving faith-statements to each other. Mark grew up, and, as with all of us, his values matured. The society around him changed with the changing times. When Mark finally got around to writing his Gospel it would have all these tints upon it. Thus, early Christians surely were correct in putting at the head of this book, The Gospel "According" to Mark. Editorial study attempts to get back to the most original accounts of the Jesus event by seeking the unmodified materials.

There are other results that have come from the scholarly study of Jesus as portrayed in the Gospels, but these three are sufficient to orient us in this brief introductory volume.

As with so many great personages of history, Jesus left no writings of his own, nor a personal diary. He did not have even one note-taker among his Apostles. In spite of all these difficulties in knowing the original Jesus, our study is worth the time and effort given to understanding this one who changed the course of history and who was the seed of the Christian movement.

The Gospel Genre

The literal translation of "Gospel" is "good news." This was not a term that the writers of the Gospels themselves used to describe their books. Later Christians attached this term because, evidently, they thought that the Gospels were presenting good news to readers.

The good news was that God acted in Jesus. Such a person in whom God acted was called a "messiah." There were many messiahs in Jewish history. Jesus was one more.

Exactly what his messianic work wrought was viewed differently by each of the four Gospels. Mark (from now on I will drop "The Gospel According to" for the sake of brevity) was disappointed that Jesus did not free Israel from Roman rule; and yet he sensed that Jesus had freed him and other believers from sin's rule. Matthew saw in Jesus the Kingdom of Heaven at hand, a completely new order beyond common political dimensions; he expected Jesus to return soon to oversee it. Luke viewed Jesus as the messiah of personal benevolence; he took a different view of the scope of history; and he extended the expansion of the Jesus movement to the entire world. John saw in Jesus a divine figure who was present with God before creation and who beamed down into history for a few years to show humans what God and good living were really like.

As to the establishment by God's direct power of a Kingdom on Earth, many must have agreed with Mark and Matthew that Jesus was coming soon, if not yet. Others straddled the issue with Luke. Others agreed with John that a coming Kingdom had to be interpreted and explained in a new way—they proclaimed the Kingdom as a messianic age which begins when one believes in Jesus and extends into eternity.

When Jesus had not returned by 70 CE, then by 80, then by 90, and then by the turn of the first century (time was not yet divided into BCE and CE, but the people of that era certainly knew what a year was) the Jesus movement was forced to take the longer view of history suggested by Luke and asserted by John. It accepted the reality of no return, but it seems to have kept an eye out just in case Jesus did appear. The point of relevance here is that when the messiah didn't return in person, it became more and more important to record and preserve the known information about him that described his significance. Congruent with this was a shifting from a relationship with Jesus as a pre-resurrection historical person—a relationship such as a Peter or an Andrew might enter as Jesus associated with them beside the Sea of Galilee and enlisted them in his mission—to an experiential belief about who Jesus as the post-resurrection Christ was.

The four Gospel writers obviously had a relationship with Jesus in at least one of these paradigms. They describe their respective relationships with Jesus in their Gospels. It is well to note that not many persons could and did write such accounts. Literacy was the ability of a few. A smaller number of people in that day could write a treatise. An even tinier minority were sufficiently bi-lingual, in the Aramaic that Jesus spoke and the Greek in which the Gospels were written, to be linguistically able to write such treatises. These four writers of the Gospels were able and were moved to write just in case Jesus did not return.

One further factor in the emergence of the written Gospels was the Jewish-Roman War 66-70 CE (Jerusalem fell in 70, but the last small Jewish outpost did not fall until 74). When it ended with a thorough Roman victory and a devastating Jewish defeat, the main stream of Jewish religion and the Jesus stream which had begun as an aspect of the Jewish religion, became separated. The two had not seen eye to eye ever since the crucifixion inasmuch as the Jewish main stream saw Jesus as not the messiah—he did not free the nation from Roman rule, nor did he establish a kingdom. The Jesus stream pictured him as a different kind of messiah. Near the close of the War a prominent main stream Jewish leader, Yochanan ben Zakkai, fled Jerusalem and set up a center for Judaism on the coast at Jamnia. The Jewish main stream busied itself with defining more exactly their religion and with making an official collection of their literature. About 90 CE they completed their literary canon known as the Bible, or to Christians as the Old Testament. Exactly what happened to the Jesus stream is not certain, but tradition says that as many of them as possible fled Jerusalem and went east across the Jordan River to the city of Pella. At Pella it is not clear exactly what happened, but the Jesus movement did survive. Perhaps from Pella and at least from other sites, certain of its members began writing a Christ-centered literature.

With this brief survey of sources we are prepared to consider each of the four Gospels for portraits of Jesus.

Chapter 5

Jesus—Mark

Introduction

The Gospel According to Mark generally is agreed to have been the first of the four Gospels written.

Of singular importance in our historical study of Christianity is the noting of the title of the book: "The Gospel According to Mark." The title states that this book is Mark's version of the Gospel. It is not the Gospel according to Jesus, or anyone other than Mark. It is Mark's faith-statement about Jesus. It is a statement of the meaning that Mark finds in Jesus. This book does not claim to be, nor is it, a book of history; hence we must draw out historical information carefully.

Since this is Mark's faith-statement, it is incumbent to find out information about Mark. Our first discovery is that there is no Mark. Nowhere in the book is the name of Mark given. The book is not signed. The first known attribution of a name was in the second century by Papias (c. 60-130), the bishop of the church in Hierapolis. He speculated that a "Mark" wrote this book and that Mark learned his stories about Jesus from the Apostle Peter. There is no corroboration extant for these claims by Papias. He gives no sources for his claims.

There could have been a Mark who knew Peter; but "Mark" was a common name in that time and nearly anyone could have known a "Mark." If the author of the book had attached a biographical note it would have saved countless historians uncounted hours of research.

Nevertheless, using the name of "Mark" for the sake of convenience, there are a few things that can be inferred about the author. He writes from a male perspective. He probably is of Jewish background inasmuch as he is familiar with Jewish things, although not intricately acquainted; consequently, he may be a Jew of the Diaspora. He is not an exclusivist Jew because he expresses no antagonism toward Gentiles. He probably is relatively young: the pace of his narrative is that of a younger man and he pictures Jesus with strength. There is no evidence that he knew the Jesus of history. Mark probably is bilingual in Aramaic and Greek; although the Greek in which he writes is rather elementary and not fluent. Presumably he translated the stories from Jesus' native language of Aramaic into Koine Greek, something that a very small percentage of the population could do; it is estimated by historians that only about ten per cent of the entire population of the Mediterranean world could write in any language.

A further inference is that Mark is in a hurry to write. He is under some kind of pressure, not named, to set down his faith-statement about Jesus. Perhaps the pressure is the culminating of the Jewish-Roman War: Jerusalem was losing, the Roman army was storming the gates and inflicting many casualties. Once the Roman army entered the city, as they were sure to do with their formidable military might, there was no telling what they would do to the city and to its great edifice, the Temple, and to any Jews they could catch.

The Jewish-Roman War was not supposed to turn out this way. The Jews who started the rebellion had a few successes in Galilee and thought they could win a war. Furthermore, their successes were such that they believed that God was fighting with them, miraculously empowering them. These rebels who were known as, or who came to be known as, the Zealots, were very religious in addition to being very warring. They were certain that God, who dwelt in the Temple, would not allow heathen Romans to conquer the holy city nor harm the even holier Temple.

As the War proceeded, the Zealots began losing. They retrenched and retrenched. Finally they retrenched to Jerusalem. In the years 67-68 CE they laid down rules for conducting battle from Jerusalem. They required all inhabitants to join them in the rebellion or risk being slaughtered on the spot for being unpatriotic Jews. Blood ran deep around the Temple courtyard and in the streets, much of it the blood of those who preferred peace with Rome. More serious yet, the Zealots defiled the Temple by chasing some of the Temple staff inside the Temple and killing them there. The Zealots' action was called by Mark and later by Matthew "abominable," "an abominable desecration." The Zealots were a minority, but they were a fierce minority who killed many of their own people.

The Roman army encamped around Jerusalem and held it in siege. They let no one enter or leave. Consequently, it is far from certain who exactly were inside the city walls at the time the siege was laid. Besides the permanent residents there may have been caravan route travelers, merchants, peasants bringing produce to market, pilgrims making sacrifices at the Temple, and the like.

Mark may have been one of those caught in town at the laying of the siege. There is no direct verification of this, but it seems reasonable to place him in such a threatening situation in the years 68-70 CE. The pandemonium, the slaughter, the blood, the stench, and the pursuit of any Jews who were reluctant to take up arms against the Romans—the Jesus Followers were known for being peace-loving and for turning the other cheek—could have been pressures on Mark to jot down fast and furiously his memoirs of a person who meant more than life to him. He writes hurriedly and possibly with regret that he hasn't written sooner. In this time of crisis he realizes how life-directing his faith in Jesus is; he strives to share his faith-statement with the rest of the world. In doing so, he brings the literary genre of "Gospel" to the Christian movement.

Other scenarios could be constructed for the setting of Mark's writing. What is certain is that he is in a hurry to record his own spiritual discovery in the face of a threat before it is too late. Mark writes with haste. He doesn't bother to mention the birth or childhood of Jesus. He begins with an adult Jesus. He piles up story upon story without transitions to connect them. He depicts Jesus as traveling from place to place rarely stopping even to eat or sleep. He ends his Gospel abruptly, in a mood of fright. At least by the year 70 he has composed the first Gospel that would become canonized.

Actually, the true author of the work, while important, was not an issue for readers in the beginning years of Christianity. They were taken by the subject, Jesus the messiah, not by whoever was the author of this book. Mark's Gospel appears to have gained widespread acceptance among readers. Apparently it agreed with the stories handed down about Jesus and with experiences the readers themselves had with him.

Outline

The Gospel According to Mark is a work about twenty pages long. It is not a neat work. Mark gives neither abstract, nor outline, nor synopsis. Scholars in the thirteenth century divided the book into chapters and in the sixteenth century divided the chapters into verses for ease of reference and study. A brief outline is: 1)ministry of Jesus, chapters 1-9; and 2)Passion of Jesus, chapters 10-16.

A more elaborate outline is:

I. Chapters 1-9:

- A. A confident Jesus sets forth to bring in the Kingdom of God.
- B. Those who repent shall enter a Kingdom status now.
- C. The Kingdom shall go forth from Galilee and spread throughout Israel.
- D. Those who really know Jesus must keep his identity a secret.
- E. Jesus' Twelve Disciples are so dense that they do not understand what Jesus' basic teachings and mission are, although the commoners and spirits do.

II. Chapters 10-16:

A. A contemplative Jesus decides that the time is right to extend his message to all Israel and goes to the capital, Jerusalem.

B. Jesus sets forth the vital qualification for good standing in the Kingdom—servanthood.

C. The dense Disciples still do not understand Jesus, nor do the regular inhabitants of Jerusalem.

D. Jesus is arrested, charged with blasphemy against the Jewish religion and sedition against the Roman state, and sentenced to death.

E. Jesus is crucified, buried, raised, and disappears from his tomb.

(The earliest copies of Mark end at 16:8. Verse 8 reflects the haste and threat already discussed—the last word of the verse is "afraid." The several alternate endings of the Gospel were added by unknown editors at unknown dates.)

Characteristics and Thesis

Since Mark is the first of the Gospels, it is important to study it carefully. Mark has come to know about Jesus as an historical person and also to know Jesus as messiah. Mark does not delineate these two aspects of Jesus; consequently we shall study Mark as a whole cloth, noting for ourselves both the "Jesus" aspect and the messiah aspect. Notable characteristics of the book are these:

1. Haste.

Mark's pace in the Gospel is hasty. He portrays Jesus as a person in a hurry. His narrative jumps from setting to setting without transitions. For persons traveling on foot, Jesus and his entourage move at an incredible pace. The haste evidently has nothing to do with the physically possible/impossible movement of Jesus and his followers; rather it has to do with Mark's situation. He considers the message contained in the events more important than the normal physical and factual aspects of the events. He has to tell others about his encounter with Jesus before he himself meets an untimely end.

2. Secrecy.

According to Mark, Jesus continually exhorts persons not to tell anyone about his identity. Scholars have struggled with this aspect which seems to be completely out of place for a messiah: surely a messiah would want to be known—why else should a messiah come? Mark's emphasis on secrecy, notably in the first division of the book, may be due to an oral tradition claim that Jesus wanted the Kingdom of God to be seen as a freely chosen commitment through repentance on the part of hearers, rather than as an irresistible thrust of power from on high. Another possible cause may be autobiographical, inasmuch as Mark himself may not have been willing or able to state publicly who Jesus was, until the latter part of the book. Another possible explanation is that Mark contrives it in order to keep the Zealots from suspecting the Jesus followers as being disloyal to the Jewish side in the Jewish-Roman War (see comments above on the Zealot edicts of 67-68 CE). Another possible explanation is that Jesus himself is uncertain about his identity; did he not pray to be released from his fate and did he not cry out to God, "...why have you forsaken me?"

3. Denseness.

Mark makes the observation repeatedly that the chosen Twelve Disciples of Jesus cannot understand even the parables that Jesus tells. Parables were a common way of teaching in that day. The crowds understand them, but the Disciples ask Jesus in private to explain them. Also, the Disciples make requests of Jesus that are out of keeping with the nature of Jesus' Kingdom: James and John request political positions and Simon Peter wants to build a Jesus shrine. Moreover, the Disciples are bewildered when Jesus talks about his impending martyrdom, the theme of the last half of the book. The attribution of denseness to the Disciples is a topic that has intrigued many scholars. After all, the Disciples were with Jesus constantly over a long period of time. They may not have had extensive schooling, but they were intelligent and able.

Mark doesn't stop with the Disciples as being dense. He includes the leaders of the Jewish religion, the Jewish nation, the rest of the world—and himself. It seems as if only demons and the commoners understand who Jesus is. Not only have all the others missed the message of Jesus, but Mark himself has not understood the nature of Jesus' messiahship in a manner that commanded Mark's entire allegiance; that is, until this moment. He wakes up as the unbelievable and catastrophic events are taking place in the sacred precincts of his own religion.

4. Galilee.

Mark sets nearly all of Jesus' ministry in the province of Galilee. It is to Galilee that the Disciples are to go after the resurrection. It is in Galilee that the ministry of Jesus will be fulfilled. Mark's selection of Galilee is plausible. If Jerusalem were in mortal danger at the time Mark wrote, then neither regular Jews nor Jesus Followers would be safe there. Also, Jerusalem was where Jesus was crucified, neither a safe nor desirable place for his followers. In addition, Jerusalem had been the locale for the arrest and the beginning of the end for the famous Christian evangelist, Paul, whose martyrdom surely was fresh on the minds of Jesus Followers. Finally, Mark may be implying that Galilee, Jesus' home province, could be the place where the "true" religion would be distinguished from the "disqualified" religion that had rejected him in the province of Judea.

5. Thesis.

The **thesis** of this brief book is stated in 10:45: **Jesus is the serving messiah.**

Commentary

According to Mark the key to Godly life is in service to others. In such service Mark saw the messiahship of Jesus.

This type of messiahship was not the kind that most Jews had expected. Mark himself labors over the identity of the Jesus whom others are calling the true messiah. Mark frequently uses the title, "son of God," but this is a title that had been applied to many people in Jewish history. It meant a creature of God, or one who acknowledged the fatherhood of God. It did not carry any necessary implication of divinity. Mark portrays the Jews as a whole, and the Disciples of Jesus, as well as himself, as being unsure of Jesus' identity; evidently all of these expected a God-sent messiah to free Israel from foreign rule and establish a new and righteous kingdom in a spectacular manner; but Jesus did not do so.

Nevertheless, there was something special about Jesus. The commoners understood this. The spirits knew this. Even the Gentile centurion at the crucifixion knew this. What they knew was a supremely good man who ministered to human needs in spite of theological speculation or political intrigue.

Mark does not accord divinity to Jesus. Mark is uncertain about Jesus' relationship to God in the usual theological terms. Nevertheless, Mark, a religiously concerned young man, saw in the stories told to him about Jesus of Nazareth the model person, a person clearly after the manner of God.

As you begin reading Mark, note that the narrative begins when Jesus is an adult. Jesus joins the movement of John the baptizer at the Jordan River several miles east of Jerusalem. John preached that the Kingdom of God was composed of those who repented of sin, believed in this Kingdom, and were baptized.

After some weeks Jesus returns to Galilee, perhaps to avoid John's fate of being arrested. He preaches in Galilee the same message as John's. Only those who are cleansed of sin may live in the Kingdom of righteousness. The Kingdom is "at hand," actually in the beginning stages, and will come fully if all will repent. Whether or not this Kingdom is a social event or an individual event is not made clear.

Jesus selects some Disciples—a practice common to teachers of that day—and begins an itinerate ministry of teaching and healing. He becomes well-known in the area around the Sea of Galilee. Mark uses the words "the whole town," or "the whole region" to show that he thought Jesus' activities were very important. Mark is extravagant with his numbers of people who gathered in Capernaum inasmuch as there were no buildings large enough to house such crowds and there were no amplification systems for the outdoors; but, again, such extravagance no doubt is to show Mark's estimation of the importance of Jesus' activities.

Mark indicates that thc healing and teaching ministries of Jesus were especially popular. Through the first division of the book—through chapter 9—Mark relates thirteen stories of healing and six parables of teaching.

Mark gives developing roles for the crowds of people: the commoners grow in astonishment, the chosen Disciples grow in bafflement, the religious authorities grow in suspicion, and Jesus' own family grow concerned about his pace and mental health.

Jesus persists, but acknowledges that few if any may understand his mission. His comments become ominous. The first division of the book ends.

The second division of the book begins in chapter 10. Jesus decides to leave Galilee and extend his mission to Judea. He advises his Disciples about the importance of serving others, even to the point of giving his life. Two of his closest Disciples still have not understood the essence of Jesus' mission to minister to the needs of individuals rather than establish a political regime; they ask for political positions, but Jesus rebukes them. The Disciples become troubled. Jesus becomes contemplative.

The next six chapters cover only one week in the life of Jesus—a week called the "Passion," and the description of it is called the "Passion Narrative." On a Sunday Jesus reaches Jerusalem. He is greeted with enthusiasm by crowds of people and escorted into town; this event is called "Palm Sunday." Just why there are such crowds is not explained logically. There are no other sources apart from the Gospels that mention such a gathering. It is puzzling that if Jesus had spent his time thus far in Galilee, how he could have such a greeting on his first day in a city a hundred miles away in Judea.

Again, it may be Mark's way of showing his estimation of the importance of Jesus.

On Monday Jesus routs merchants and money changers from the Temple precincts. Actually these persons performed a service to pilgrims who came to the Temple to make sacrifices and offerings by having animals and the correct Temple tax available; it may be that Jesus thought they were conducting tourist traps, and/or that he thought the Temple should concentrate on prayer rather than sacrifices and offerings. It is surprising that no authorities stop Jesus or arrest him.

On Tuesday Jesus spends a long day teaching at various sites in Jerusalem. His topics include prayer, authority, taxes, commandments, stewardship, and others.

On Wednesday Jesus spends the day in the nearby town of Bethany at Simon the leper's house. Judas Iscariot, one of the Twelve Disciples, makes a deal with the religious authorities to "betray" Jesus; what may be the case is that Judas Iscariot thinks of the Kingdom of God in political terms and hopes to force Jesus, whom he sees as having extraordinary power and charisma, into the action that the Jewish mainstream expected of a messiah.

On Thursday night Jesus observes the Passover Festival with his Disciples, and perhaps others, in a traditional Seder meal. Afterward he adjourns the group to the Garden of Gethsemane, a park-like area across a small valley from Jerusalem. There Jesus prays fervently that God will relieve him of the consequences of his servant role. God is silent. Judas comes to identify Jesus. Jesus is arrested and tried. He fails an interrogation on orthodox religious belief and behavior by the high priest and is condemned on a charge of blasphemy; he acknowledges that the terms "son of God," and "messiah" apply to him.

On Friday Jesus fails an interrogation on political issues by the governor, Pontius Pilate, and is condemned on a charge of sedition; Jesus' admirers are acclaiming him as "king" of the Jews and Jesus does not deny the title. According to Mark, Pilate is not convinced of Jesus' guilt.

Pilate thinks he could acquit Jesus and save face if he offers to release either Jesus or a very infamous murderer named Barabbas (note that this name means "Son of the Father/God"; what an irony!). Pilate apparently hopes that the crowd will clamor for the release of Jesus. Not so. The crowd calls for Jesus' crucifixion, a call just as puzzling as why there was a crowd at all on Palm Sunday. Pilate accedes.

Jesus is executed by crucifixion—the method accorded to non-Roman citizens (the citizen form would have been beheading, and the Jewish form, if there had been no Roman involvement, would have been stoning). The place of execution is called "Golgotha," or "Calvary." Jesus is put on the cross at 9 a.m. At 3 p.m. he addresses God and asks why God has forsaken him. God is silent. Jesus dies in an unusually short time for a death by crucifixion.

Joseph, a Jew from Arimathea, and a member of the Jewish high council, the Sanhedrin, secures permission to bury Jesus quickly since the dead are not supposed to be left outside during the Sabbath, which would begin near 6 p.m. Jesus is taken to a crypt, apparently somewhere near Jerusalem rather than ten miles away in Arimathea, and interred; it is so late in the day that there is not time to embalm him with the customary spices and oil.

As to Saturday, Mark is silent.

On Sunday morning some of the women go early to embalm Jesus. Instead of finding Jesus, they find a young man sitting in the crypt who tells them that Jesus has been raised and is not there. The young man says that Jesus is returning to Galilee. He tells the women to go tell the Disciples. Instead of following orders, the women flee in terror and say nothing to anyone. The Gospel, in its oldest copy, ends abruptly.

Chapter 6

Jesus—Matthew

Introduction

The second of the four New Testament Gospels is The Gospel According to Matthew.

Matthew's Gospel—"good news" about Jesus—gained widespread acceptance in the Jesus movement probably because it agreed in large measure with Mark and because it added information, especially information at the beginning and the ending. Matthew used Mark as a guide, but had at least two other sources of information about Jesus.

As with Mark, also, the title was added later, "The Gospel According to…."

As with Mark, we need to devote some time to learning about the author. The earliest record of naming an author comes from a second century Christian, Bishop Ignatius of Antioch, who thought that a "Matthew" wrote it. Ignatius' comment came to light about 110 CE. He and others linked Matthew to the Matthew/Levi of the Twelve Disciples of Jesus. There is no historical record to support this linkage. "Matthew" was a common name in that time.

Some information about the author can be inferred from his work. Matthew is a male. He is an accomplished scholar of the Jewish religion, perhaps a rabbi, at least a practicing member. He is well acquainted with the Jewish scriptures and quotes them frequently. He uses the Jewish terminology of Kingdom of "Heaven" rather than the terminology Kingdom of "God," which means that he was stricter in his religious orientation than Mark; the use of "Heaven" avoided saying "God," which name very religious Jews would not speak. He writes with the air of a learned professor. He writes in Greek, as did Mark, but his prose is much more sophisticated. His Gospel is like a teaching document, well-organized, well-written, and inclusive of the entire life of Jesus. He has an authoritative air, as if he is used to associating with the ruling class. Consequently he would be at least middle-aged and probably older. He is a person of faith in Jesus as the messiah, and shares his conviction in a written record.

Unlike Mark, Matthew appears to be in no great hurry to write his book. The threat to life and limb is not present. He makes little note of the Jewish-Roman War, the destruction of Jerusalem, or the rebuilding of the city, which may mean that he writes from outside Israel. One tradition claims that he wrote from Antioch in Syria where the Jesus Followers were first called "Christians." The Church in Antioch was strong and could have furnished Matthew the security and resources for writing his Gospel.

The dating of this Gospel probably is about 85 CE. The reasons for this dating are several. Matthew was written after Mark, whose book was in writing probably by 70. Matthew uses the term "church" that had not been in vogue yet when Mark wrote. The institutionalizing of the Jesus movement into the church apparently came after Mark's writing. By 85 the church certainly had become separate from the main stream Jewish religion; the destruction of Jerusalem in 70 was a huge separating factor. Furthermore, Matthew drops the expectation of the immediate second coming of Jesus, which had been a cardinal belief in the early Jesus movement. Further still, the good news of Jesus is, according to Matthew, being preached widely in the Mediterranean world. Matthew does not mention the destruction of Jerusalem and the Temple specifically, although 22:7, 21:41, and/or 24:15-16 may refer to it. Evidently the events of 70 were long past.

Matthew, then, gives us a later view of Jesus and the Christian movement. He speaks of the synagogues as "their" synagogues: Jewish religious leaders declared about the year 85 that Jesus Followers were anathema and were not to be permitted the use of synagogues. The Pharisees, who were the sole surviving Party of the Jewish religion, are made by Matthew into the arch enemies of Jesus and the Jesus Followers; the Pharisees were the ones who composed the above anathema against the Christians. A date later than 85 is not probable inasmuch as Emperor Domitian's move against Christians is not mentioned by Matthew; that move began when Domitian ascended the throne in 86.

Matthew writes his Gospel in a year of calm. There is no imperial threat. There is no local threat. It is reasonable to assume that he is writing from outside Palestine at a site where materials about Jesus were available for his scholarly research. He writes a complex, polished, personal faith-statement in the Jesus whose brief career culminated in his crucifixion fifty-five years earlier.

Outline

The Gospel According to Matthew is a work about thirty-five pages long, almost double that of Mark. As with Mark, it was divided into chapters and verses centuries later for reference and study. Unlike Mark, Matthew gives multiple outlines of his work. In general he follows Mark's chronology, but adds material to it.

The simplest outline of Matthew would consist of three headings: 1)childhood, chapters 1-2; 2)ministry, chapters 3-20; and 3)Passion, chapters 21-28.

A more detailed outline could be:

I. Chapters 1-2:

- A. A true Jewish messiah, Jesus, is born, as attested by his genealogy.
- B. Jesus is adored by wise men.
- C. Jesus' life is threatened, but his family escapes with him, and they relocate from Judea to Galilee.

II. Chapters 3-20:

- A. Jesus teaches about righteousness.
- B. Jesus teaches about discipleship.

C. Jesus teaches about the Kingdom of Heaven.
D. Jesus teaches about the church.

III. Chapters 21-28:
A. Jesus tries to teach in Jerusalem.
B. Jesus confronts implacable opposition.
C. Jesus is executed.
D. Jesus is raised from the dead.
E. Jesus returns to Galilee and commissions his Disciples to go into the entire world, make disciples of all nations, and teach them to observe all of his teachings.

Characteristics and Thesis

As with Mark, a way of studying Matthew is to concentrate on main characteristics:

1. Best law interpreter.

Matthew portrays Jesus as the best interpreter of the Jewish Law. Jesus, as a conscientious Jew, accepts the Law of God, but interprets it at certain points in ways that more nearly fit his times. Matthew acknowledges Moses as the messianic lawgiver in days of old; but Jesus is the messianic lawgiver in the new age. Matthew often mentions that those who heard Jesus exclaimed that he taught as "one having authority!" Matthew shows Jesus interpreting the Law with a depth beyond that of the Torah of old. According to Matthew, Moses was good, but Jesus is better. Jesus is so good that God claims him as his own from the very start of Jesus' career at his baptism. Those who truly listen to Jesus' interpretations are "amazed."

2. Ideal king.

Matthew portrays Jesus as the ideal latter day, completely without sin, king. Jesus is from the line of David, but a greater than David. Matthew exalts Jesus beyond the common terminology, "son of God," used by Mark, which referred to humans as God's creations. Jesus is accorded all the regal power to avoid suffering and death, but Matthew portrays Jesus as willingly accepting the Passion in order to fulfill the highest Jewish aspirations. Matthew seems to accept the designation which Jesus seemingly acknowledged when questioned by Pilate, "King" of the Jews.

3. Superlative teacher.

The Gospel According to Matthew presents Jesus as the superlative teacher. The Gospel is pedagogical through and through. From the very first of the book, it is not shepherds from the lowest class of people, but sages from the wisest class of teachers in the world who come to pay homage to Jesus.

Matthew's work is presented in textbook fashion. It has a Prologue, 1:1-4:22. It has five divisions which set forth Jesus' interpretation of the Law: Book I, 4:23-7:29; Book II, 8:1-11:1; Book III, 11:2-13:53; Book IV, 13:54-19:2; and Book V, 19:3-26:1. It has an Epilogue, 26:2-28:20. Matthew has other divisions that cut across the first divisions, but which do not interrupt or contradict the first divisions: 1)the age of John the Baptist, a good age but not the final age; 2)the age of Jesus, a better age but not the final age; and 3)the age of the church, the best age because it is the culmination of the others.

According to Matthew, Jesus goes beyond previous teachers by using parables to describe righteous living and the nature of the Kingdom of Heaven—parables which even the commoners can understand. Chapters 5-7 are the collected teachings of Jesus. So superb are these teachings that Matthew stages them on a mountain—that is, on a high point on Earth, a point that is the nearest to Heaven.

4. Fulfiller of scripture.

Matthew is unique in citing so many passages from the Jewish scriptures (what Christians now call the Old Testament, but at the time of Matthew, the only scripture either Jews or Christians had). Matthew quotes thirty-five biblical passages: ten from Isaiah, seven from Exodus, six from Deuteronomy, five from Psalms, three from Hosea, and one each from Leviticus, Malachi, Micah, and Zechariah. Matthew uses all of these to support his claim that Jesus is the messiah of God who fulfills the scriptures.

5. Thesis.

The **thesis** for the Gospel According to Matthew is spread all over the book. It is telegraphed in the visit by the wise men. It is inherent in the "Sermon on the Mount." As with Mark, Matthew is not concerned with the historical details about Jesus—his looks, personal quirks, attained age, eating habits, finances, nor the kind of rock on which he sat for his teaching Sermon. The thesis of Matthew's work is this: **Jesus is the teaching messiah.**

Commentary

The Gospel According to Matthew was authored by one who found the key to Godly life in the teaching of Jesus. In turn, Matthew expresses the obligation of himself and all who follow Jesus to relay that teaching to others.

Matthew goes beyond the uncertainty of Mark about the identity of Jesus. Matthew is certain that Jesus is the ideal in all respects. Matthew traces Jesus lineage directly back to the progenitor of the Jews, Abraham. Matthew presents Jesus in full Jewish context as the perfect messiah. Matthew attributes to Jesus the skill of a law interpreter, the authority of a king, and the wisdom of a teacher; all of these are based on the parenthood of Abraham who was the original messianic figure commissioned to be a blessing to the entire world. According to Matthew, Jesus fulfills all of the above roles and goes beyond his predecessors in quality. Matthew does not call Jesus divine, but he comes close. At least he takes a step beyond Mark and declares that Jesus is the finest of all the messiahs.

One of the reasons that Matthew ties Jesus so closely to the Jewish progenitors may be because Rome did not like new religions if they contradicted traditional religions or claimed to have the only god to the exclusion of traditional gods; such new religions would cause conflict and upset the *Pax Romana*. If Matthew could show that the Christians were the true Israel, then they would be within an established religion. Rome actually was rather tolerant of Judaism and made special concessions to the Jews.

For the study of Matthew, it can be read word for word, but that may not be necessary if Mark has been studied carefully. Approximately six hundred of the six hundred, sixty one verses in Mark are found in Matthew. It may be sufficient herein to comment only on those passages that differ from Mark or which are not contained in Mark.

The first two chapters of Matthew give material not found in Mark. They begin with the genealogy of Jesus, traced from Joseph back to Josiah to David to Abraham. Joseph, David, and Abraham may be familiar persons; Josiah was king of Judah in the seventh century BCE, one of the "good" kings, who became famous for "finding" a copy of the Law of Moses in a Temple remodeling project. His rediscovery of the Law was a messianic event in Judah and brought about a renewal of commitment to YHWH and to religious worship. Matthew states that he has found fourteen generations between these groups of ancestors—and he is almost, but not quite, an accurate mathematician. The number fourteen probably has to do with a numerical equivalence derived from the name of David—DVD equates to 4+6+4=14. While Matthew traces Jesus' lineage from Joseph, he does not name Joseph as the biological father of Jesus; instead Matthew asserts that Jesus was fathered by the Holy Spirit.

Matthew describes Joseph and Mary as being betrothed, a relationship that was stronger than our engagement, but not yet a sexually consummated relationship. Mary shows pregnancy, which causes Joseph consternation; but he spares Mary the dire consequences of "dismissing" her—a woman so dismissed would be unwanted by any other man, would have to find support from relatives or earn a living through indentured slavery or prostitution. Joseph spares Mary these indignities.

Matthew begins quoting scripture in the first chapter to support his belief that Jesus is the messianic figure to reveal the righteousness of God. He continues quoting regularly throughout the book.

Matthew places the birth of Jesus during the reign in Israel of King Herod the Great. Since Herod died in 4 BCE, this would place Jesus' birth about 7-4 by taking into account the journey of the wise men and Herod's "slaughtering of the innocents." (The numbering of years by a Christian monk many centuries later was intended to place Jesus' birth at the year zero, and the monk was almost right.)

According to Matthew the holy family are residents of Bethlehem, a small town a few miles from Jerusalem. Sometime after Jesus' birth they are visited by the wise men, are made aware of Herod's intent to eliminate competitors for the throne, and are directed to flee to Egypt. They do so. After Herod's death, they return "from out of Egypt," ala Moses and the Exodus. They do not return home because Herod's son and successor in Judea, Herod Archelaus, appears to be a threat of some kind to young Jewish males. The family resettles in the village of Nazareth, Galilee, over which ruled the more lenient son of Herod, Antipas.

The story of Jesus joining John the Baptist's movement is similar to Mark's account. In Matthew's opinion the baptism of Jesus is support for his claim that Jesus is the messianic figure who will bring in the new kingdom of righteousness like unto Heaven. Matthew minces no words in calling the past claims of righteousness in Israel inadequate; these old claims will be cut down and burned, perhaps implying an analogy between the destruction and burning of Jerusalem and the Temple.

In the fourth chapter Matthew states that Jesus leaves his childhood home in Nazareth, probably a village that archaeologists say had only a few hundred population, and makes Capernaum his new home and the headquarters for his mission.

Chapters 5-7 show Matthew's composition and writing at their very best: the "Sermon on the Mount." Matthew in the immortal language of the "Beatitudes," the "Golden Rule," and other prose, describes the Kingdom of Heaven. He has Jesus vowing that true righteousness is measured by performance, not by mere profession.

Through chapter 20 Matthew makes some minor additions to Mark, such as the healing of two blind men, instructions to his followers on how to act when assisting in the carrying out of his mission, and an invitation to all the weary to find rest in him. Matthew continues by relating the sign of Jonah, the temptation of unclean spirits to return and bring colleagues to a cleaned house, more parables about the Kingdom of Heaven, and a teaching about the proper payment of the Temple tax. He mentions the "church" as if it is a firmly established organization.

Then the Passion narrative is begun by Matthew. One of the notable features is the pronouncement of woes upon the scribes and Pharisees. As noted earlier, such pronouncements probably are the result of antagonisms that arose years after the death of Jesus when the Pharisees and the Jesus Followers had serious disagreements.

Matthew gives a long paragraph to the fate of Judas Iscariot. Judas is remorseful, tries to return the money to the authorities, and finally commits suicide.

In the last chapter, Matthew gives variations from Mark on the death, resurrection, and post-resurrection appearances of Jesus. Matthew tells of an angel in the empty tomb, rather than Mark's young man. Matthew tells of Mary Magdalene and the other Mary meeting Jesus face to face outside the tomb, rather than women fleeing the empty tomb in terror. Matthew gives details about the raised Jesus' return to Galilee.

In a forceful liturgical summary/conclusion, which had been developed by the church over the decades, Matthew describes the ideal Jesus as giving a "Great Commission" to his followers: to make disciples of all nations; to baptize believers in the name of the Father, Son, and Holy Spirit; and to teach the baptized all the ways of righteousness. In closing, Matthew quotes a statement of assurance from Jesus: "Remember that I will be with you to the end."

Chapter 7

Jesus—Luke

Introduction

The Gospel According to Luke generally is agreed to have been the third of the four Gospels written.

Luke's Gospel was accepted by the Jesus movement apparently because it agreed with Mark and because it added information not in Mark or Matthew. Luke uses Mark as a guide, may have Matthew at hand, and uses his own sources plus an independent source, called "Q" (short for "Quelle") that Matthew, but not Mark, had. Luke does not claim historical accuracy; all he claims is that he has a faith-statement to make about the person and work of Jesus. We shall examine the work for historical information anyway, for there are gleanings to be found.

As with Mark and Matthew also, the title was added later, "The Gospel According to...."

As with Mark and Matthew, the name of this Gospel does not appear in the book. The name comes from second century Christians. One record states that the influential Bishop of Lyons, Irenaeus (c. 130-c. 200), in 190 CE thought that a "Luke" wrote it. Some in Irenaeus' time linked Luke to the profession of physician because of the tone of the book, and then linked the physician to the Apostle Paul because in one New Testament book there is a reference to a Luke as being a physician and Paul's traveling companion on a single occasion. There is no other support, however, for these second century assertions.

From the book we can infer considerable information about the author. Luke probably is a male—"probably," because of all the Gospels, this one has such tenderness and compassion that some scholars have claimed that it was written by a woman. This claim is supported by passages such as the birth story, Mary pondering in her heart, Mary and Elizabeth meeting, Jesus at age twelve, the sisters Mary and Martha, the outcasts, the Prodigal Son, the widow's lost coin, and the like. A wide variety of names have been advanced as possible authors, ranging from Mary Magdalene to the Syrophoenecian woman who convinced Jesus to let the "dogs" (Gentiles) have the crumbs under the (Jews') table. Very few scholars agree, however, that the author was a woman.

Luke's ethnic identity is a moot issue. On the one hand he is familiar with some things Jewish. On the other hand he sounds very much like a Gentile. In any case, Luke is acquainted with a variety of nationalities and identifies himself with no specific national or ethnic group.

Luke is a compassionate person. He is interested in the tender experiences of life. He appears to be older than Mark, but younger than Matthew. He claims to have done extensive research before writing in order to pen an "orderly account" so that readers may "know the truth." This claim has raised some scholarly eyebrows, wondering whether Luke meant that the other Gospels were not orderly and/or were not true. He writes in Greek, as do Mark and Matthew. His language is fluent and engaging, indicating that Greek is at least one of the languages native to him. Whether or not he is fluent in other languages is not known.

Luke is less versed in the scriptures than is Matthew. Luke is neither in a rush nor under threat as is Mark. The date of Luke's Gospel is about 90 CE. He has taken time, probably years, to research the materials for writing about Jesus. He has come to accept that Jesus is not coming again, soon at least. He addresses his book to "Theophilus," which may be a name, but which is a generic term meaning "God-lover"/"Loved of God." If the name is meant to be generic, then Luke is addressing his Gospel to Gentiles since "Theophilus" is strange to Jewish communication; if so, this shows that the Christian movement has had time to move rather fully into Gentile circles. This possible address to

Gentiles is buttressed by Luke's story of the Good Samaritan, an oxymoron term in Jewish opinion. A further reason for a later date than Matthew is that Luke relates the story of the two men of Emmaus who suddenly realize the identity of Jesus in the "breaking of bread"—Luke implies that his readers will realize the effectiveness of breaking bread with Jesus, which is to say that the Lord's Supper/Communion is so well established among Jesus Followers that the readers will catch a deeper significance beyond merely three men eating dinner together.

The place of writing of Luke is uncertain. It is where materials about Jesus had been collected. It is a place where the Christian movement is under no threat from Domitian's persecution—the persecution apparently was not empire-wide. The book sounds as if it could have originated in Alexandria. The library there was the best in the world. Scholarship was encouraged. Many religions were represented there, including the Roman, Greek, Jewish, and possibly the Buddhist; so that in an atmosphere of tolerance the persecution of Christians by Emperor Domitian may not have been carried out in Alexandria. There is, however, no definitive information on the location. At best it can be said that the writing did not take place in Israel or Syria.

What is certain is that Luke makes a concerted attempt to placate Rome and keep on its good side. He insists that Jesus is innocent of sedition against Rome. He extols Christianity but keeps it within the authorized framework of Judaism in order not to offend the political authorities. He makes no reference to the destruction of Jerusalem and the Temple so that there can be no inference made about Roman guilt. He does not tout the soon and revolutionary coming of the Kingdom of God; instead, he invites readers to imitate the compassionate Christ in their daily living.

Outline

The Gospel According to Luke is a work about the same length as that of Matthew. Such a length would have been about the maximum for a scroll or a codex in that era. It is a gathering of material moreso than an "orderly account" as the author claims, unless by orderly he means that Jesus was born, lived, and died. There are no overt or covert outlines in the book.

Our short outline of Luke is: 1)childhood, chapters 1-3; 2)ministry, chapters 4:1-to 19:27; and 3)Passion, chapters 19:28-24:53.

A more detailed outline is:

I. Chapters 1-3:
- A. Two messianic figures are conceived and associated in their careers, John the Baptist and Jesus.
- B. Jesus' birth is celebrated by shepherds and angels.
- C. Jesus is circumcised as an infant, presented in the Temple when coming of age—twelve.
- D. The ancestry of Jesus goes back through Adam to God.

II. Chapters 4-19:27:
- A. Jesus confidently begins his ministry in spite of temptations to do otherwise, and in spite of opposition at home.
- B. Jesus selects Disciples, conducts a Galilean ministry.
- C. Jesus, his Disciples, and mission teams make a series of campaigns of teaching and healing in order to increase faith.
- D. Jesus extends his ministry to Samaria and Perea.

III. Chapters 19:28-24:53:
- A. Jesus extends his ministry to Judea, but weeps over Jerusalem because of probable rejection.
- B. Jesus acknowledges rejection, prepares his Disciples for his demise, institutes the Lord's Supper.
- C. Jesus is executed, forgives his executioners.
- D. Jesus is resurrected, makes appearances in and around Jerusalem.

E. Jesus ascends to Heaven from Bethany, Judea, directs his followers to wait for "power from on high" to be given to them by God for the carrying on and carrying out of his mission.

Characteristics and Thesis

As with the previous Gospels, a way of studying Luke is to concentrate on its main characteristics:

1. Compassion.

Luke begins with a tender story and doesn't change. Event after event in Luke is related with such tenderness, such compassion, such concern for the outcast, that the mood of this Gospel is noticeably different from the others. A classic example of this is his description of Jesus' birth: swaddling clothes, manger, no place in the inn, shepherds adoring, angels singing—all told with a gentleness that has inspired the writing of countless Christmas carols in the succeeding centuries. Even the name "Luke" is more relaxed than in-a-hurry "Mark," and more congenial than in-a-classroom "Matthew."

2. Universal.

Luke constructs a genealogy for Jesus that goes back not just to Abraham, as in Matthew, but all the way back to God. It has almost no resemblance to Matthew's genealogy of Jesus, but it fulfills Luke's universal motif: Jesus is more than Jewish, Jesus is Gentile, too; and more so, Jesus is the universal One from God. Luke acknowledges no provincial or national boundaries for God's compassion. He addresses his book to a probably generic Theophilus—anyone who loves/is loved by God. Luke gives special attention to the outcast, the common, and the hurting, and also does not exclude the in, the up, and the healthy—he includes all.

3. Innocence.

According to Luke, Jesus is not guilty of the charges brought against him. Jesus is not a blasphemer, as the Jews charged; rather Jesus is the universal messiah not bound by any ethnic or national strictures. Jesus is not a seditionist, as the Romans charged; rather Jesus is a messiah of righteousness, and not a political pretender or a military revolutionary.

4. Autonomy.

Luke portrays Jesus as being in charge of his own coming and going. According to Luke, neither the Jews nor the Romans, nor anyone else, controls the destiny of Jesus. Luke goes beyond Matthew a bit, and way beyond Mark, in placing Jesus very close to being divine; at least Jesus is sired by God's Spirit. Luke illustrates this with comments he alone records as coming from Jesus on the cross: "Father, forgive them…," "Today you will be with me in Paradise," and "Father, into your hands I commend my spirit." Luke does not have Jesus suffering while on the cross. Jesus is in charge. Jesus is the supreme prophet who knows how his own story shall come out; and God does not disapprove.

5. Thesis.

The **thesis** for this magnetic human interest Gospel involves compassion. Luke points out, from the birth of Jesus to the Good Samaritan to the Prodigal son to the criminal on the cross, the constant love of divine behavior. Luke has Jesus loving others so devotedly that any consequences, even crucifixion, can be worked into the equation. The certain thesis of Luke is: **Jesus is the compassionate messiah.**

Commentary

The Gospel According to Luke sees the divine in terms of the greatest of the commandments, the love of God expressed through loving others. Luke presents this as the meaning of life, the reason for being, and the key to Paradise. Luke goes beyond the uncertainty of Mark about the identity of Jesus, and beyond the ideal man of Matthew. Luke traces Jesus right back to God. It isn't necessary for Luke to have Jesus establish a separate Kingdom at any Earthly location; he cites Jesus as saying, "The kingdom of God is among you." Luke's faith is not in a messianic kingdom, a political kingdom, even a religious kingdom; instead it is in a kingdom of compassion. Compassion is the behavior of God toward humanity, and Luke shows it to be the proper behavior of human to human. It is as if Luke cuts all the hampering strings everywhere in life, and joins all human hands in a clasp with the divine.

For the study of Luke, it can be read word for word, but that may not be necessary if Mark and Matthew have been studied carefully. Comments are in order for those passages that differ from Mark or Matthew, or are not mentioned by them. Keep in mind the main characteristics of Luke's Gospel named above. They are keys to an understanding of the book.

Luke begins his Gospel with a prologue. He dedicates his work to a "Theophilus," who could have been a benefactor, although the name could have been a generic term. He declares that his account is the result of extensive research into the stories about Jesus and that his account is the orderly and true one.

He relates the meeting of Mary with a kinswoman, Elizabeth. Both are pregnant, Mary with Jesus (the messiah); Elizabeth with John (the Baptist). Both Mary and Elizabeth have been divinely impregnated: this is, of course, a means of impregnation few women would claim in our day, but in the days of old it was not uncommon for male gods to have children by human mothers. Mary sings a song of praise for the good her child might bring to the world, the "Magnificat." Elizabeth's husband, Zechariah adds a prophecy of hope about John, the "Benedictus."

This Gospel presents a unique birth story about Jesus. Luke's story has no threat of King Herod, no wise men coming, and no implication that the holy family resides in Bethlehem. Instead, Luke declares that Mary and Joseph live in Nazareth and go to Bethlehem near the time of delivery for Mary in obedience to the Caesar Augustus, Octavian, who has issued a decree for a census of every inhabitant for tax purposes. Luke states that everyone everywhere has been ordered to report to everyone's ancestral cite to register. Luke places this during the regional governorship of Quirinius who had jurisdiction over Syria and Israel.

This census raises huge questions, such as how millions of people could all at the same time traverse distances across the Roman world (or who would be left at home to tend the shops); how they could know the homesite of their ancestors countless years, maybe thousands of years, before; or why there is no such census mentioned in official Roman chronicles. Luke raises dating problems in that Quirinius is known from extra-Gospel sources to have been appointed governor in 7 CE. If Luke's story is "orderly" and "true," then Jesus would have been born eleven to fourteen years later than Matthew states, and would have been in his late teens or early twenties when he died. Evidently Luke wants Jesus to have been born in Bethlehem regardless of chronology.

The mood of the birth story is very different from that in Matthew. Luke's version has the flavor of the common people. Mary has to travel near the height of pregnancy, either walking the hundred or so miles from Nazareth or riding on a jolting donkey. There is no room in the inn when Mary and Joseph arrive in Bethlehem (although one wonders why they didn't seek out relatives such as Zechariah and Elizabeth). A number of shepherds leave their folds (tending flocks at night was not the usual practice) and come to worship the newborn Jesus—shepherds were about the lowest class of workers in Israel, the class of the Am Ha-ares, not the learned class as in Matthew.

Luke interpolates information about John and Jesus; then indicates that John and Jesus have matured at about thirty years of age and are pursuing their callings. Luke then sets forth his version of the genealogy of Jesus. It is so strikingly different from Matthew's genealogy that no final explanation of the difference has been found. Luke's genealogy has seventy-seven ancestors, while Matthew's account has forty-one. Luke's genealogy goes back to God, indicating that Jesus is a world citizen from the start; while Matthew's account only goes back to Abraham, the father of the Jews, indicating that Jesus is a Jew before he is a world citizen. Both Luke's and Matthew's genealogies appear to have been composed to support their own theological biases.

The Gospel According to Luke has some material not found elsewhere. Luke has a story about the raising of a widow's son from death at Nain. Luke records a grateful statement about the women disciples of Jesus financing the food and lodging for Jesus' entourage. He relates the account of an unwelcomed visit to Samaria.

In addition, Luke presents two unforgettable parables. The first is the "Good Samaritan" in chapter 10. The parable is the result of a conversation between Jesus and a lawyer about how to inherit eternal life. When the lawyer presses a fine point, Jesus broadsides him with this parable on loving the needy. Jesus applies the parable in no uncertain terms to the lawyer, "Go and do likewise."

Luke's second unforgettable parable is that of the "Prodigal Son" in chapter 15. It follows short parables on lost sheep and lost coins. There are two lost sons in the feature parable, each lost for a different reason. The parable is so true to life and so deeply true to life that it may have happened again yesterday. The two lost sons come out at different conclusions. As with the Good Samaritan parable, you should read this Prodigal Son/s parable from the source in order to get its full impact.

Luke relates an incidental story in chapter 19 about a rich man, Zacchaeus, who is short in stature, but who is looking for something in life beyond his wealth. He climbs a tree to get a good look at a person who is offering that something. He is surprised when Jesus looks at him and then calls him down to a path beyond his wealth that leads to salvation. Luke implies that such salvation is open to the entire world.

The last portion of Luke's Gospel is the Passion narrative. Luke generally follows the account of Mark. A Lukan addition is the claim that Jesus is innocent of blasphemy and sedition, the charges that were used to condemn him to death.

In chapter 23 Luke gives three "words" from the cross, statements by Jesus, that are found in no other Gospels. Luke cites them to show that Jesus is autonomous, that Jesus is in control of his fate and merits final rest in the good hands of God.

Luke's resurrection stories are different from those of the other Gospels. Luke records none of the fright in Mark, and none of the demanding commission of Matthew. Luke alone tells the story of the two men who count themselves as disciples of Jesus, walking on the Emmaus Road, talking about the events of the Passion Week, but not understanding the outcome. They had hoped that Jesus was the messiah to redeem Israel, but Jesus was taken out by execution. Jesus appears incognito beside them and explains at length that his career is in keeping with the whole history of Israel. They are grateful and invite Jesus to be a guest in their home. During dinner, Jesus takes bread, blesses it, breaks it, and gives it to them. At that moment they realize who their guest is.

Before they can say more, Jesus vanishes from their sight. They rush back to Jerusalem, tell the Apostles what has happened, and—surprise again—Jesus appears in their midst. Luke makes a point of Jesus' real presence by telling that Jesus eats a piece of broiled fish. Jesus tells them again why the Passion is part of the divine plan for repentance and forgiveness of sins to all nations. Then he tells them that they are to be witnesses to all these things. They raise no objections. Jesus promises them a clothing of power from on high. Then he leads them to the suburb of Bethany, blesses them, and is carried up into Heaven. They worship, return to Jerusalem, and bless God "continually in the Temple." They do not go to Galilee, as Mark hopes and Matthew avers.

Luke's avowed careful selection of materials undoubtedly reflects what is meaningful to him. The human interest stories are his delight, rather than Mark's ceaselessly rapid performance of good works, and rather than Matthew's stream of authoritative teachings. Luke sees "messiah" as the One who really cares about every individual no matter what is his or her Earthly status. The person addressed at the beginning of the book, Theophilus, is everyone, for everyone is "Loved of God."

Chapter 8

Jesus—John

Introduction

The fourth of the four New Testament Gospels is The Gospel According to John.

John's Gospel was accepted by the Jesus movment for reasons that are not entirely evident. It is unlike the other three Gospels in many ways. It has a different beginning. It has a different chronology. It has a different way of designating the wondrous works attributed to Jesus. It has differences in theology. It has differences in form. The list could continue.

What we can say is that it was written at a time in the history of Christianity when its message was needed. This, coupled with the popular, if erroneous, belief that it came from one of Jesus' Twelve Disciples, resulted in its inclusion in the canon of the New Testament.

As with the previous Gospels, the title of this work was added later, "The Gospel According to...."

As with the previous Gospels, the name of this Gospel does not appear in the book, but comes from second century Christians who thought that a "John" wrote it. "John" was a common name in that era; there are several Johns mentioned in the New Testament, including one of the Twelve Disciples of Jesus. About the year 180 CE Bishop Irenaeus (c. 130-c. 200) of Lyons claimed that John the Disciple of Jesus wrote this book. Irenaeus claimed that John lived to an exceedingly old age in the city of Ephesus.

This claim cannot be substantiated, however. In fact, three famous and prolific writers earlier than Irenaeus—Justin Martyr, Polycarp, and Ignatius—make no mention of John being in Ephesus or of writing this Gospel. In addition, the book of Acts states that John of the Twelve Disciples was illiterate, which makes his writing of John quite unlikely. Furthermore, since the Gospel was written in Greek rather than in the Aramaic spoken by the Disciples, the unlikeliness is increased greatly.

There is a reference in chapter 21 to the "disciple whom Jesus loved" as being the one telling and writing the stories about Jesus, but it does not go on to claim that this beloved disciple is also the author of the Gospel. Indeed, there is some doubt that chapter 21 was part of the original Gospel; chapter 20 gives a perfectly good conclusion to the book.

Since The Gospel According to John is a personal faith-statement we shall try to discover who the author was in order to see more clearly his stance. In the process of considering John we may be able to find further information about Jesus.

The author of this Gospel undoubtedly is male. He is a Christian. He knows about some aspects of Christianity in considerable depth. He is acquainted with Greek, Gnostic, and Mystery religion thought, a further mark of considerable learning. He is older rather than younger. He is more interested in metaphysical rather than historical meaning. His omission of two commonly used terms in that time does cause us to pause, however; he does not mention "apostle" or "church." Perhaps he didn't know any apostles and so thought them to be peripheral, but the apostles were accorded the highest respect by everyone else. Surely he knew about the church unless he were totally isolated or totally out of touch. In one of the tables at the back of my book there is a list of known church congregations by the year 150 CE; the list is lengthy and names many geographical locations. In addition, the term "church" is used by other Christian writers in the last quarter of the first century and following when speaking about the Christian movement.

There is no indication in the Gospel that the author knew Jesus in person. Actually, there is material in the Gospel concerning Jesus that probably is historically inaccurate. For example, while the other Gospels have Jesus going to Jerusalem only at the end of his ministry, John has Jesus going there three times. Whereas the other Gospels have Jesus being arrested on the night of the Passover, John has him arrested on the night before the Passover. Whereas the other Gospels call Jesus' miracles straightforward "works," John calls them merely "signs." These and other passages lead to the conclusion that John did not know about the Synoptic Gospels, or didn't care. The latter is possible inasmuch as we have noticed that the Synoptic writers were concerned more for the spiritual meaning of Jesus than the historical facts about Jesus; perhaps John was just more radical on this point.

The author of John appears to be under no pressure to write a Gospel, except the desire to make his faith-statement. The place from which he writes has been guessed at with about the same prolificacy as there are scholars. It would seem that a place in Asia Minor would be likely, or Alexandria would not be out of the question, cities where there was extensive familiarity with things Greek and Hellenistic; but surely it would not have been written from the same city as the other Gospels. The book has the flavor of speaking to a community of Christians who are trying to separate themselves from Judaism on the one hand and from Gnosticism on the other hand, not just physically but also theologically.

The date of the writing of John can be determined in this way. Second century Christians were of the same mind that it was written later than Mark, Matthew, and Luke. If that is the case, then the earliest date would be after 90 CE. A further consideration for a date after 90 is that John has given up entirely any belief in a second coming of Jesus. Such a belief was so strong among early Christians that it would have taken many years for it to have been discarded completely. John translates the second coming into the coming of the Holy Spirit, the Paraclete/Advocate. In addition, John is hostile toward the Jewish authorities; such hostility was a growing Christian phenomenon beginning late in the first century. Another consideration is that there are allusions in the Gospel to Gnostic and Docetic ideas about Jesus; such ideas began circulating late in the first or early in the second century.

The latest date for the writing of John is 140. A fragment of a copy of the Gospel has been found in Egypt, a fragment called "Ryland's John" after the finding archaeologist; the fragment has been dated between 130 and 140. A probable date, therefore, lies between 90 and 140, and can be narrowed slightly to 100-120.

Outline

The Gospel According to John is a work longer than Mark and shorter than Matthew and Luke. As with the other Gospels, it was divided into chapters and verses many centuries later for ease of reference and study. A short outline of John is: 1)prologue, chapter 1:1-18; 2)ministry, chapter 1:19 to chapter 17; 3)Passion, chapters 18-20; 4)epilogue, a probable later addition, chapter 21.

A more elaborate outline is:

I. Chapters 1:1-18:

- A. Jesus is portrayed as being fully divine, with God from the beginning.
- B. Jesus is portrayed as coming in the flesh to carry out God's long range plan for humanity.

II. Chapter 1:19 to chapter 17:

- A. Jesus is proclaimed as the Lamb of God.
- B. Jesus selects Disciples.
- C. Jesus begins performing signs that demonstrate his divine status.
- D. Jesus attends the Passover festival in Jerusalem, cleanses the Temple.
- E. Jesus proclaims that it is through faith in him that God gives eternal life.
- F. Jesus ministers in Samaria on his way back to Galilee.
- G. Jesus continues doing signs and wonders to demonstrate that he is the eternal light, bread, way, truth, shepherd, resurrection, vine, and the like.

H. Jesus travels to Jerusalem for Festivals, engages Pharisees and others in debate.
I. Jesus attends Pesach/Passover Festival, gives long discourses and prayers on eternal concerns.

III. Chapters 18-20:
A. Jesus is arrested in Jerusalem.
B. Jesus is tried and convicted.
C. Jesus is crucified, buried, and rises.
D. Jesus appears to his Disciples and convinces them of his resurrection.
E. Jesus is unequivocally announced as the Messiah and Son of God.

IV. Chapter 21:
A. Jesus makes further post-resurrection appearances.
B. Jesus queries Peter about Peter's love for him.
C. A great many works about Jesus are acknowledged by the beloved disciple.

Characteristics and Thesis

A way of studying John is to delineate its main characteristics. With these in mind it may be easier to appreciate the book as a whole.

1. Timeless.

There is little demarcation of time in John between the here and the hereafter. The word "eternal" is continually used: it is a Greek concept, not a Jewish one, meaning that which is "forever in both directions." It seems as if John is asserting that there never was a time of creation, but that the universe is since always. While the Jews thought in terms of death and resurrection, or in no immortality at all; while the Greeks thought that the soul—the essential identity of a person—always lives; John asserts that everyone who believes in Jesus as the Christ already lives forever and never really dies.

The practicability of this assertion of John, however, raises its own set of problems. Perhaps it is John's way of gently disclaiming that Jesus would return to Earth and establish some kind of national state in Israel as the Kingdom of God. More strikingly, perhaps it is John's way of disclaiming a Heaven. Perhaps it is his way of claiming that the eternal way of God, the eternal way of the Logos, the eternal way of the cosmos itself, is to enter a relationship of loving trust with the ultimate reality of the universe. Such a relationship constitutes eternal life; it can begin now and it lasts forever in principle.

2. Esoteric.

John's Gospel wafts into space from time to time. It was written when esoteric elements were of increasing influence in the Christian movement. Those who championed esoteric elements agreed with other Christians that God was spirit, but they took this belief to the extreme. They claimed that since Jesus was divine like unto God, Jesus must have been spirit, too. (Even to our day the Spirit of God is called the Holy "Ghost" by some Christians.)

One such theology which capitalized on the esoteric element was called "Gnosticism." The Gnostic Christians made a radical separation between this material world and the other spiritual world. Since humans were of this world, they were separated from the true world/reality/God. They should try to get out of this material world and try to get back into the spiritual world from which they came; not that they should commit suicide, but that they should shun all things material. Furthermore, the Gnostic Christians held that Jesus must have been completely spiritual since to have been material in any degree would have made him less than fully divine. If Jesus had been material then he would have been corroded in nature and corrupted with sin.

One of the subsets of Gnosticism was Docetism, which held that since God could not be incarnated in a human, because that would tarnish God, the divine Jesus only appeared to be human. He wore a human mask much as a ghost in our time has to wear a bed sheet in order to be seen. Jesus was an apparition much as we might create virtual reality on a computer. Moreover, there was no way that God could be killed on a cross or otherwise, and still be God.

Both Gnostics and their subsets were confessing Christians. They gradually grew in strength in the developing church. They probably had a swell of growth after Emperor Domitian began prosecuting Christians in the 80's and 90's, which prosecution made the spiritual realm even more attractive than the material realm.

The Gospel of John lends itself to esoteric interpretation. It speaks nowhere of any human or physical needs of Jesus. It has only two limited expressions of emotion by Jesus. John describes Jesus as fully divine. John avers that Jesus is not a recent Bethlehem-born child of God—there is no birth story at all in John—but is eternally with God, meaning that forever Jesus is. Besides, while on earth, Jesus is in charge of his entire mission, rather than being subject to human, Earthly, material, political, or religion forces. He decides when the time is right to do whatever; he directs the events of his trial and execution.

Having noted all of this, John at the same time hastens to point out that the Word/Christ/God did "become flesh," and "dwelt among us." It is as if John wants it both ways. He is not willing to concede the day to a strictly esoteric view, even though he is esoteric in passage after passage. He also insists on "flesh" in other passages. It seems that the making of a distinction between the divine and the human, between the spiritual and the material, between the other world and this world is enigmatic.

3. "L" words.

In The Gospel According to John there is distinctive use of "L" words:

a. Logos.

The writer of John was aware of the Greek philosophical talk that began six centuries earlier with Heraclitus, who called the ultimate principle of the universe the "Logos." This term is translated variously as reason, expression, word, or logic. John uses the term and assumes that his readers will understand what he means. The Logos gives existence, order, and meaning to all things. John gives a twist to the term and declares in his prologue that Jesus himself is the Logos. John claims that the Logos is incarnate in Jesus. Divinity is shown in the flesh so that human beings might see the nature of divinity, yet the Logos retains eternally divine identity.

b. Light.

The writer of the Gospel According to John is familiar with the philosophical thought from Alexandria that divinity exudes light. John declares that God sent light into the world and that Jesus is the light of the world.

c. Life.

John makes no distinction between this life and the next. Somehow a non-believer is not in the true stream of life until that person believes in Christ; then the person exists eternally.

d. Lord.

John uses this title for Jesus. It was a title used by many Jews who thought that the name of God, as well as the word "God," was too holy for human lips to speak; therefore, the word "Lord" was substituted.

e. Love.

John's famous verse in chapter 3 is that "God so loved that world that he gave…." The supreme lifestyle is love, as God loves and gives, and as Jesus loved and gave himself on the cross.

4. Allegory.

John constructs his work so that many of his words have two meanings, literal and spiritual. The world understands the literal, but the followers of Jesus understand the spiritual. For example, at the wedding celebration at Cana, the host literally has only water left, but Jesus transforms it into spiritual wine—that is, from the common water of Earth into the best drink the guests ever had, the wine of Heaven. Or for example, later in the Gospel, Nicodemus understands what being born is, but does not understand what being born again is. John's stories all are meant to be signs that the spiritual transcends the literal.

5. Thesis.

The **thesis** for the book of John involves the spiritual rather than literal. There are several passages that reflect this: "…and the Word was God"; "I am..."; "I and the Father are one"; and the like. John's thesis is about the identity of Jesus: **Jesus is the eternal Messiah**.

Commentary

The action of The Gospel According to John moves from the divine scene to the human scene to the divine scene. While on the human scene, John goes beyond the serving thesis of Mark, the teaching thesis of Matthew, and the compassion thesis of Luke. John transports the reader into the spiritual realm with long discourses and prayers. John attempts to translate what the Word must have known since the beginning of all creation. John has no doubt that Jesus is the messiah, and he treats the office as if it has a capital "M." He ignores any connection of the Messiah to politics. He pays meager attention to the relationship of the Messiah to Jewish interests. He uses his own themes, rather than those of the Synoptics. His is a Gospel apart from the others, termed through the ages as the "Fourth Gospel."

For the study of John, it could be read word for word because it is so different. On the other hand, it shan't be read with haste. Many find that reading it as devotional literature is best; certainly it is not meant to be an historical treatise. There are some passages that are akin to those in the Synoptics that will not be mentioned herein. Otherwise, a few comments about what is distinctive may be helpful. Remember that the Gospel is highly allegorical as contrasted with literal.

John sets the tone of his Gospel at the very start. He personalizes the Greek concept of Logos, which the Greek philosopher six centuries earlier, Heraclitus, probably meant was an intelligence rather than a person; John expands the word by making "Logos" a fully divine person. He identifies it with Jesus. John proceeds to make Jesus absolutely significant: Jesus is eternal life itself.

In John, Jesus crosses paths with John the Baptist, but there is no record of Jesus being baptized; instead the Baptist is in the story, it seems, merely to announce the identity of Jesus.

The Gospel of John relates two miracles, or signs as he calls them, that also appear in the Synoptics. He relates six that are not in the Synoptics. The six unique ones are in 2:1, water to wine; 4:46, healing of the nobleman's son; 5:2, healing of the lame man at Bethzatha; 9:1, healing of a man born blind; 11:1, raising of Lazarus from the dead; and 21:4, the catch of fish. The turning of water into wine is intrinsic to the Gospel. The water that the Jews used ceremonially, such as at a wedding, is turned into the best wine by Jesus. Water and wine both were symbols of life, but wine the more exquisite. Jesus is the converter of life from what is, even from that which is good, into the very best: the best comes to humanity in Jesus/Messiah/God.

There are no parables in John.

The cleansing of the Temple comes at the beginning of John, rather than at the end as in the Synoptics. John treats it as an event of enlightenment and revelation, rather than one of judgment as do the Synoptics. The symbolism is that the old Temple must give way to the new temple—Jesus himself; it is okay if the old Temple is destroyed even, because it would make the rising of Jesus as the true temple even more dramatic. The true temple is one not made by hands. Some scholars have suggested that John places the Temple incident at the beginning of his Gospel for the same reason he places the miracle at Cana at the beginning—to assert that Jesus the Christ is in charge. Jesus demonstrates his divine authority from the very beginning.

The Samaritan woman at the well is one of the spiritual allegories. Jesus is the living water, the real life, the spiritual life, the divine life, the eternal life. If the woman drinks of this she will taste true life and never again thirst.

The raising of Lazarus from the dead is a literal story, but with spiritual meaning. One of the surprising points of the story is that Jesus is notified of the sickness of Lazarus, but does not go to him immediately. Instead he tarries until Lazarus dies! Jesus then tries to instruct the crowd about the spiritual meaning of this incident, but the crowd is slow to comprehend; so slow that Jesus gets impatient, one of the two times he shows human emotions in John, and "snorts like a horse," the Greek says. Evidently the crowd's weeping over a physical loss got to Jesus who was the spiritual life, the very life of all creation. The Life was right in their midst and they knew it not.

The point of John's signs has been speculated on by scholars. It may be that John's point is that faith is a life-style, a mood, an esoteric awareness, rather than an assent to historical events. God incarnating is an eternal process, not a chronicle. God is the presence of grace beyond and yet within everyday events. This makes all life anywhere sacramental, a sign of the "presence-ing" of God eternally. Eternity is not a Heaven, but the everlasting present. Since God is always enfleshed, all of the blessings of God are in the eternal present. Any thought about a Kingdom of God out there in some future time on foundations of expensive jewels misses the point: rather, the very presence, the fullness of God is now. It is incarnate in Jesus, the eternal Messiah.

Later in the Gospel, Jesus begins talking about his Passion. He says that the hour for it has come, and he says it as if he is in charge of the timetable. There is no Garden of Gethsemane pleading or shedding of great drops of blood. Jesus directs all the events of the Passion. The soldiers who come to arrest him cannot do so until Jesus gives the word. Jesus controls his appearance before Pontius Pilate. Jesus orchestrates his own scourging; it is not part of the death sentence as told in Mark and Matthew. On the cross Jesus gives his own body permission to die. He chooses when to die; he is not killed. The cross is Jesus' dais of lordship, not an ignominious rood. The cross is a sign, a sign of being "lifted up." At the end, Jesus, as if surveying the whole landscape, looks out and pronounces, "It is finished."

John speaks of the coming of the "Paraclete." His meaning of Paraclete seems to be the abiding presence of God in the world after Jesus has departed. The Paraclete apparently is John's substitute for the second coming of Jesus. There is no second coming of Jesus; there is the Paraclete, the continuing presence of God in the world. A second coming of Jesus is not necessary since the Paraclete is the same presence of God as if Jesus were on Earth (exactly what this presence is or does is not clarified by John; such words as "love" or "good intention" may be appropriate).

The resurrection is the greatest sign of exaltation of the status of Jesus. John seems to mean that both Jesus and those who believe in Him shall never die even when opponents behave at their worst. The appearance to Mary in the garden is occasion for John to declare that what people should hold/hug, is not a body that they can see and touch, but the spiritual body, the eternal body, the Logos. John ends the saga by bringing his Gospel full circle back to his prologue.

The epilogue (chapter 21) almost certainly is a later addition to The Gospel According to John. Many justifications have been advanced for this addition. One is that the epilogue was added to justify why the author of the book physically died, after having stated over and over in the book that eternal life begins at belief and never ends; 21:23 is an obvious attempt to put a spin on the author's death. Neither this nor the other justifications have been universally accepted by scholars; maybe at best we simply can say that the epilogue is there. The epilogue concludes with the immodest claim that there were so many other things that Jesus did, that if every one of them were written down, the world itself could not contain the books.

Whether The Gospel According to John ends at chapter 20 or chapter 21, the thesis still stands: Jesus is the eternal messiah. Jesus is the full expression/logos/presence of divinity. Jesus and God, thus, are one; and all who believe in Jesus, who enter the Christ-Way, are in—within—that eternal dimension of God.

Concluding Word about the Four Gospels

1. Likes and Differences of the Synoptics and the Fourth Gospel.

a. Ministry.

In the Synoptics Jesus' ministry lasts less than a year and is conducted mainly in Galilee; in the Fourth Gospel his ministry lasts several years and is conducted mainly in Jerusalem.

b. Stories.

In the Synoptics the stories are short and pithy; in the Fourth Gospel they are long and involved.

c. Theme.

In the Synoptics the central theme is the divine kingdom come/coming to Earth; in the Fourth Gospel it is eternal life.

d. Signs.

In the Synoptics there are miracles; in the Fourth Gospel there are signs.

e. Exorcisms.

In the Synoptics there are frequent exorcisms; in the Fourth Gospel there are no exorcisms.

f. Lord's Supper.

In the Synoptics the Lord's Supper is on Passover, one night later than it is in the Fourth Gospel. The Synoptics probably are right since three of them agree; whereas John has in mind from the beginning of his Gospel that Jesus is the Lamb of God, and the lamb for the Passover is killed the day before the Passover.

g. Identity.

In the Synoptics Jesus' identity is made problematic by his refusal to perform miracles or give signs in order to exhibit divinity; in the Fourth Gospel Jesus gives signs and lengthy discourses to prove his divinity.

2. The Nature of Jesus in the Four Gospels.

The Gospels give us four versions about the nature of Jesus ("Christology") in the time between the crucifixion and the following ninety years—29/30-120. The Gospels are the records about Jesus that were finally accepted and approved by the dominant stream of Christianity.

Mark, closest in time to Jesus, written about 70 CE, asserts that Jesus is an extremely good Jewish man. Mark appears to include himself in the company of those who expect God to send a human messiah who will be the founder of a new Kingdom on Earth, a Kingdom ruled by Jesus and/or the Twelve Disciples.

Matthew raises the estimate of the messiah from a temporal level to that of the ideal. He places Jesus in that role as the ideal Jewish man who is divinely sired. Matthew shies from locating the Kingdom of Heaven on Earth. One of the causes for this is that Jesus has not come again. The early-expected second coming of Jesus has not occurred by 85 CE. Matthew makes an adjustment to that expectation.

Luke adds that Jesus is a more than a human messiah and more than any other Jewish messiah: Jesus is universally good and divinely sired (but, remember Mary is human). Luke portrays Jesus right at, but not into, the divine level by asserting that Jesus is very nearly in complete control of his Passion. Luke has a touch of hesitation about the divine status, such as when he relates that Jesus agonizes in the Garden of Gethsemane about his impending death; nevertheless, Luke ends with the conviction that Jesus is more than mortal. Luke has Jesus demonstrating on the cross that the Kingdom of God is a present Paradise which the compassionate inhabit—the compassionate, whether messiah or criminal. Luke does not dwell on the topic of a second coming.

John completes the process of divinizing Jesus. John has no miraculous birth story and no transfiguration for Jesus: they are not necessary because John views Jesus as already divine—divine forever. He seems oblivious to the earlier concept of a national, physical, political, all-encompassing, ideal Kingdom of God being miraculously sent to Earth. In chapter 18 he quotes Jesus as saying and repeating that the Kingdom is not of this world; rather the "Kingdom" is the eternal envelopment of God around those who willfully enter it through the Christ-like door of love.

3. The Historical Jesus.

Many scholars have devoted their lives to the study of the historical Jesus. This quest for the historical Jesus was the title of a landmark work by Albert Schweitzer in the early twentieth century. In it he acknowledged the difficulty for us moderns to discover who the historical Jesus was. His conclusion, however, is an echo of the four Gospels. Their writers agree and disagree on historical data. Their writers each put in some and leave out some. They bequeath partial information to us.

In the end, the Gospel writers go beyond the historical Jesus to the Jesus of their faith. They write from the standpoint of having been transformed spiritually by Jesus, rather than from a modern historian's yearning for at least enough information to paint on canvas—or in words—a photo-like portrait of Jesus. It can be said that their faith-statements are what has made their literature immortal. (But I still wish they hadn't been so parsimonious with their historical data about Jesus!)

Now we continue in our study by finding out what happened to the Jesus-inspired movement that was founded and developed in his name after his Earthly life.

Part III

Christianity

Chapter 9

Christianity—Founding

The Acts of the Apostles

Introduction

The work which describes the founding and early years of the Jesus movement is called "The Acts of the Apostles."

The title of this New Testament book promises much. It would tell us of all of the activities of all of the Twelve Apostles of Jesus. Were this the case, our knowledge of beginning Christianity would be broad indeed. Alas, the work relates some of the acts of some of the Apostles, John and Peter especially; then it relates the acts of Paul who was not one of the Twelve Apostles at all, but who calls himself an Apostle. Thus Acts is a helpful but incomplete guide to the activities of Jesus' chosen ones.

An explanation of the limited delivery of Acts is in order. What happened to this book is that it was written without a title; years later the title was added. The later composer of the title is responsible for over-labeling the book. In spite of this blemish, the book of Acts provides invaluable historical information for our study.

It tells us of the founding of the Christian movement. It tells us of the determination of the founders to spread the good news about Jesus in the face of formidable opposition from the established religions' authorities. It tells us of the conversion and work of the incomparable evangelist, Paul of Tarsus. It tells us many details about the development of Christianity in its passing comments. It tells us that

Christianity succeeded because of the acts of some very remarkable people.

The author of The Acts of the Apostles is unknown. Second century tradition credited it to the same author who wrote The Gospel According to Luke. Acts seems to be a second volume of Luke; we shall accept it as such, and speak of the author as Luke, even though, as noted in the study of the Gospel, the actual author is unknown.

Some information about the unknown Luke can be inferred from the Gospel and Acts. Luke quite probably was a male. He was one who recommended unlimited measures of compassion for others. Luke appears even more like a Gentile in Acts than he does in his Gospel. He was acquainted with a variety of nationalities and identifies himself with no one specific nationality. He claims to have done extensive research before writing in order to set forth a correct account. He wrote in Greek, which implies that he was bilingual and comparatively well-educated. He refers to the Jewish scriptures, but in a more superficial manner than would a trained scholar. Luke knows basic information about Jewish history, the Kingdom of God, and the messianic hope. He respects the Law and the Prophets of the Jewish religion.

The date of the writing of Acts appears to be connected to the writing of the Gospel. If the Gospel were finished about 90 CE, then Acts soon would follow.

The author asserts that he has had time to research the materials about the Christian movement. He has accepted that Jesus is not coming again soon. He has seen the message of Jesus preached around the Mediterranean world. He has seen the movement being organized into the structure called the "church." He assures his readers that he is giving them an accurate and authoritative account of the beginning and development of the church. (The term "church" is given immediately to the Jesus movement by Luke. He does not use the term "Christianity," nor is "Christianity" used in any of the New Testament books; the date as to when "Christianity" was used is uncertain, but it has come to be equated with the religion based on Jesus, and is a virtual equivalent of "church.")

The author addresses Acts to "Theophilus," as he does the Gospel, which may be a name, but which is also a generic term meaning "God-lover"/"Loved of God." Such a term is more appropriate for a Gentile to wear than it is for a Jew. If it is meant to be generic, then Luke is addressing Acts to any Gentile who is God-loving; yet the language of Luke is universal in nature so that anyone, including Jews, would have been included because they were God-loved.

Luke writes about events between the years 29/30 and about 65. Since he wrote in the 90's, he probably would have been too young to have known Jesus personally. He may have known some of the Twelve Apostles, although this is not certain. He does not give a bibliography with Acts: we do not know from where he gets his information. Furthermore, we do not know how he is able to quote speakers verbatim when he was not there to hear them. We cannot confirm that the way in which he describes the founding and development of the church is accurate, although it does seem to be generally in keeping with the testimony of the other writings in the New Testament. The one place it disagrees with the other books is concerning the activities of Paul. Acts and Paul's letters do not agree always on details of Paul's itinerary and experiences, but they do agree that Paul plays a significant, even pivotal, role in the development of Christianity.

What can be claimed about the books of Acts for sure is that Luke writes what he deems to be important. He writes what is significant not only to the Jesus movement but also what is significant to him as a member of the Jesus movement. Acts is both historical and autobiographical.

The place of Luke's writing is uncertain. It would have been where materials had been collected. It would have been a place where the Christian movement was under no threat. Acts sounds as if it could have originated in Alexandria or in any of several of the larger cities around the Mediterranean coastline.

Outline

In brief, Acts states that the proclamation of Jesus as Messiah (Luke now accepts a capital "M") began as a miraculous event at the first Shavuot/Weeks/First Fruits of Harvest/Pentecost Festival (May/June) following the death of Jesus in 29/30 CE. It tells how the Jesus followers organized into the church. It describes how the Gospel and the church could not be stopped by various oppositions, but expanded from Jerusalem, to Judea, to Samaria, to Mediterranean areas, and finally to Rome. Acts ends when Paul reaches Rome in the 60's.

An outline of The Acts of the Apostles could be:

I. Chapters 1-8: Mainly in Jerusalem.
- A. Jesus gives final instructions to the disciples, ascends to God.
- B. The Apostles choose a replacement for Judas Iscariot, Matthias, in order to comply with Hebrew history's number of twelve tribes/territories/rulers.
- C. The Holy Spirit descends on the disciples, empowers them to preach; the result is the founding of an organized Jesus sect of Judaism, the church.
- D. The disciples continue the mission of Jesus.
- E. The first officers of the church, "servers," are chosen.
- F. The first martyr of the movement is made, the server Stephen.

II. Chapters 9-28: Elsewhere.
- A. Saul/Paul is introduced as a threat to the church.
- B. Peter welcomes Gentiles into the church.
- C. Saul/Paul is converted, becomes a missionary for the church.
- D. The Jerusalem Conference rules that Gentiles are welcome in the church without becoming full-fledged Jews first.

E. Paul is arrested in Jerusalem, is subjected to a series of trials.

F. Paul appeals his case to the Emperor, is sent to Rome, placed under house arrest, but continues to make converts for about two years.

Characteristics and Thesis

For the study of Acts, these are characteristics to be noted:

1. God.

Acts states that both Peter and Paul, the two main preachers, start their messages by attributing all power to God. God is creator. God is sustainer. God is director of history. God is the sender of Messiah Jesus. God is the redeemer of the repentant. God is the determiner of when the Kingdom of God will come and what it will be like.

According to Acts, the power of the one and only living God is the message that first must be preached. This God is the one about whom the Hebrews/Jews have been talking from of old; this God is not new, but the original, only, eternal God. The reason God has to take such a precipitous step as sending Jesus to announce the Kingdom of God is that humans have disobeyed God from the beginning and need the extra impetus Jesus gives; if humans will repent and obey God by trusting Jesus they will enter the soon-to-be-established Kingdom of God.

2. Messiah.

Acts asserts that Jesus is the Messiah (Greek, "Christ"). True, Jesus did not fulfill the Jewish hope in the realm of politics, but Jesus has a greater agendum than mere politics. Jesus is the instrument of God to establish the Kingdom of righteousness on Earth. Jesus lived and was crucified (innocently), but was vindicated as the Messiah by God's raising him from the dead and seating him beside God in Heaven. This simple message may sound like foolishness to some, says Acts, but it is the wisdom of God. The author of

Acts maintains that Jesus is innocent of the charges of blasphemy and sedition. Jesus and the Jesus movement are not public enemies, either of religion or of the state. Jesus Followers are sincere lovers of God (perhaps in a play on the recipient of Luke's works, "Theophilus").

3. Church.

The narratives in Acts are about the establishment of churches from Jerusalem to Rome. The first major event in Acts is the founding of the very first church in Jerusalem. That was a stupendous day on which three thousand members were received. While this huge number may be something of a preacher's hyperbole, it does indicate that there was a major happening. In the rest of the book, the writer traces the founding and sustaining of local church after local church.

It is important to remember that churches at the beginning were not like churches today that stand on the corner of Main and Third Streets. There were no church buildings. The Followers met wherever they could find space. In Jerusalem it may have been on a corner of the Temple courtyard (the courtyard was huge, about twenty-six acres) since there was no other place in the city for such a crowd. The many churches attributed to the work of Paul had no buildings, and may have been unable to meet in public buildings because of unfavorable public opinion. Instead, they met in members' houses, which meant that most of the churches were small groups of people who could fit into someone's house. For example, the church at Thessalonica probably had two or three dozen members when Paul left it to fend for itself; the church at Corinth probably had a few more members; but in each case the historical information we have leads us to believe that the members met in someone's house, or in several houses. Some houses had courtyards in which persons could meet.

4. Universal.

Acts has a definite plot: the Gospel of Jesus is meant for all peoples in all nations. Acts gives a progression from Jerusalem, to Judea, to Samaria, to the rest of the Mediterranean world, and finally to the capital city of Rome. It is not stated what the completion of this route means, but it well may be that the author of Acts optimistically expects the completion to bring about the establishment of the rule of God on Earth.

This route further emphasizes that the Christian movement and Judaism effectively have separated. The separation was made formal in the 80's and 90's CE when the Jews anathematized Christians and canonized their Bible (the Christians accepted the Bible as scripture, but reinterpreted it in Christological terms and called it the "Old Testament"). The writer of Acts tries to show that the Christian Way is not a new religion, but, contrary to Jewish leaders' opinion, the true religion intended by God from of old. Boldly the writer asserts that the Christian Way will accomplish what a parochial Judaism did not, could not, do.

5. Thesis.

The **thesis** of Acts is: **God is establishing the Kingdom among the obedient.**

At the start of his book, Luke sets a time table for the establishment of the Kingdom: it will happen after the Gospel has been preached from Jerusalem, to Judea, to Samaria, and finally to Rome. Luke knows that the Gospel has reached Rome. He knows that his favorite character, Paul, expects to be alive when the Kingdom comes.

At the time Luke writes—about thirty years after Paul's death—he knows that Paul has died and that a miraculously-delivered, physical Kingdom has not come. Luke appears to be in a quandary. He does not attempt an explanation of the non-coming of the Kingdom. He simply ends his book. Apparently he believes that the church will become world-encompassing; but this should have happened during Paul's activity, and it did not. Luke stops writing. He appears to be changing to the view that the Kingdom of God to come is none other than the church expanding to become world encompassing.

Commentary

The Acts of the Apostles continues the action of The Gospel According to Luke. The setting is not in Galilee, as some of the other Gospels assert, but in Jerusalem, Judea. Luke chooses Jerusalem apparently because in his mind there is a plot that must be followed: the Jesus movement must begin in the center of Jewish life, then proceed to the other provinces, and then to the rest of the Mediterranean world. This means that it is vital to show that the Christian Way is not a new religion, but is the historic religion that God began with Abraham and is now bringing to completion. Besides, an old saying in Judea was, "What good can come out of Galilee?" Galilee had as many Hellenists and Gentiles in it as Jews; therefore, how could anything authentically Jewish come from there?

The Disciples are told by the resurrected Jesus that he must leave, but the Holy Spirit will be sent to empower and embolden them. Jesus will return when God so decides to send him back to rule over the Kingdom of God on Earth. While the Disciples are waiting, they choose Matthias to replace the deceased Judas Iscariot as the twelfth Apostle—twelve was the ancient tribal number in Jewish history. There were other disciples present: women, Mary, Jesus' brothers, and one hundred twenty others.

Approximately fifty days after the crucifixion, at the pilgrim festival of Pentecost, the Holy Spirit arrives and inspires the Apostle Peter to preach the founding sermon of the church. He preaches that God sent Jesus as Messiah, that Jesus' execution was an act of disobedience toward God by the authorities in charge of capital punishment, but that God has raised Jesus as a vindication of him as Lord and Messiah. When the crowd asks what they can do about it, Peter invites them to repent and be baptized to show their desire to obey God. Acts states that three thousand persons accept the invitation. Thus the church is founded. Soon Peter preaches a second sermon and the number of adherents rises to five thousand men, not counting the women or children. Whether or not there were as many as three thousand and five thousand is a moot question, inasmuch as there are no verifying records. These numbers seem exaggerated and may be intended by Luke to say that the beginning of the church is of great significance.

Of further significance is the activity of the church. Acts 2 notes that the new converts meet daily, participate in teaching, fellowship, the breaking of bread, and prayers (critically, a much too rigorous schedule for thousands of members with no meeting, eating, or worship facilities; and the seven servers chosen a bit later would have to wait tables at an absolutely frantic pace; but let us acknowledge the intended message that something significant is happening). Moreover, the members put their money into a common treasury for the use of any as they have need. In Acts 5 is the account of two members who are not honest in the matter of sharing their money and are struck dead on the spot.

The term "being saved" is used in chapter 2. The term refers to being made fit (a process) for the Kingdom which God is establishing.

Peter and John preach, perform miracles and healings, are imprisoned and released.

As the church grows in numbers there is need for formal organization. The office of table servers and/or funds supervisors is created; seven are chosen to fill that office (they are not called "deacons" yet). Soon one of them, Stephen, is arrested. When he is given a chance to defend himself he preaches the same basic message that Peter gave, but he does so in such vehement terms that he is stoned to death—the first martyr of the Jesus movement. Saul/Paul was present and gave his consent to this stoning to death of Stephen.

The church scatters into other parts of Judea and into Samaria—in line with Luke's plot for the spread of the Gospel. Philip goes southwest to Ethiopia. Someone takes the Gospel north to Damascus, Syria, because Saul/Paul heads that direction to hunt down the Jesus followers there and eliminate them. On this foray to Damascus Paul (he had two names: Hebrew "Saul," and Roman/Latin "Paul") sees a vision of Jesus and hears words from Heaven that convince him that he should be helping the Jesus movement, not hindering it. Paul soon begins evangelistic work on behalf of the movement.

Evidently there is some uncertainty as to what to call the Jesus movement. "Way" was a popular term. Other early names were "Jesus Followers," "Followers of the Way," "Messiah People," "Galileans," or "Nazarenes." At some point in time before the writing of Acts, the name "Christian" was used in Antioch, Syria. Probably it was used in derision—those "Christ-ians!"—but the Jesus Followers liked the name and began claiming it. The term "church" is used regularly.

Meanwhile, Peter has a vision which convinces him that Gentiles are as entitled to hear the Gospel as are Jews.

Acts continues by noting that the Apostle James is martyred.

Paul continues his preaching journeys with a companion, Barnabas. At Iconium these two are called "Apostles." Also there they establish the second office that continues to be filled in the church, "elder."

"Judaizers," that is, Christians who believe that Gentiles first must become practicing Jews before they can become Christians, follow Paul and Barnabas and contend with them. Paul and Barnabas return to Jerusalem where a Conference is held about the year 49 CE to settle the matter of conditions for Gentile membership. The Conference is ruled by James, a brother of Jesus. The outcome is that Gentiles may become full members without becoming full Jews first; the only stipulations are that Gentiles must abstain from things sacrificed to idols, fornication, meat that is strangled, and consuming blood (such dishes as blood pudding were eaten by some Gentiles, but Jews viewed blood as the sacred life-giving substance given by God and belonging to God alone).

Paul and Barnabas separate and form two traveling teams. Acts follows the career of Paul. He evangelizes in many cities north and west of Israel.

Luke mentions a few further facts about church life. The churches meet on the first day of the week. They meet to "break bread," the exact meaning of which is uncertain, whether it means the Lord's Supper or congregational dinners, or both.

Paul returns to Jerusalem to deliver an offering from the churches in response to a drought in Israel. He is arrested on false charges and is tried in several courts. The Jews plot his death. The Roman governors do not expedite his case. He appeals his case to the Emperor—a privilege of a Roman citizen, and Paul was such. He is sent by merchant ships to Rome. There he is placed under house arrest while awaiting trial. He waits two years during which time he continues preaching and taking care of correspondence.

Acts ends abruptly. The fate of Paul is not known. There is a tradition that he was executed by Emperor Nero in 64/65 on a general charge against all Christians in Rome that they started the great fire in that city, which purportedly was started by Nero himself in order to clear a large area for public buildings and his own palace. Exactly why Acts ends without an ending is open to conjecture. It was written much later than 64/65, so the author was not put to death with Paul. One opinion is that Luke's plot was complete—the Gospel had traveled from Jerusalem to Rome. Another opinion is that the Kingdom of God would be completed soon in its full dimension and there was no need to write further. Another opinion is that Jesus brought the Kingdom of God in his first appearance—the church. Another opinion is silence.

Conclusion

In summary, Acts sets a plot and follows it carefully: the Gospel/good news of the activity of God leading to the establishment of the Kingdom begins at Jerusalem and expands to the capitol of Luke's world. Although the book is entitled "The Acts of the Apostles" and begins with the Apostles, it soon narrows to follow Peter and John, and then constricts to follow Paul. In doing so, it tells no more about the Twelve Apostles, but it declares that Paul is a special

Apostle who is the central figure in the development of Christianity.

Even if Paul is the exemplary Apostle, Luke doesn't deify Paul. Luke dwells on the powerful work of God to complete the plan of salvation which God has designed from the beginning of time. That plan was demonstrated and validated by Jesus, the Messiah. It is in process of being completed—by God, albeit through human Acts. Luke writes no more.

Others do write, and lead us further in the development of Christianity.

Chapter 10

Christianity—
Early Development

Introduction

The part of the New Testament immediately following The Acts of the Apostles consists of correspondence. It continues the history of the development of the Jesus movement, although in no neat manner.

Nine "Letters" or "Epistles" could be placed in this correspondence. These could be divided into early and later. The correspondence about the early development of Christianity treated in this chapter are 1 Thessalonians, 1 Corinthians, 2 Corinthians, and Galatians, all probably written during the years 50 to 55 CE.

The correspondence tells of specific and general issues that a growing Christian movement faced. This correspondence is often called "occasional letters" inasmuch as the letters address identifiable occasions of need in the churches.

We shall study them in their probable chronological order. The letters will be treated briefly. Each of the letters should be read in full at a single sitting.

1 Thessalonians

The first correspondence to be saved for posterity is a letter entitled 1 Thessalonians. The occasion for the writing of this letter is about who will be in the Kingdom of God. The coming of the Kingdom was expected to be soon, but some Christians have died and the Kingdom has not come. Will they be in it, or will the Kingdom be composed only of those who are still alive?

The letter states that Paul, Sylvanus, and Timothy are writing in answer to this Thessalonian concern. Just who did how much writing, whether Paul dictated and one of the others wrote, or whether it was a group letter, is not made plain. Most scholars assume that Paul was the "author" in one way or another—at least it can be said that Paul was the leader of this missionary team. The date of writing probably was 50-52 CE.

Thessalonica was a medium size city and the capital of the province of Macedonia. It was named after the daughter of King Philip. It had contingents of several Mystery religions, a temple to the goddess Roma, and at least one Jewish synagogue. The Christian church there was founded by Paul's missionary group. The conditions of the founding are given in variant versions by The Acts of the Apostles and Paul's letters, but in any case there was a church there.

At that time the church was a "house church," that is, it had no building but met in the houses of members. (All of the churches in the first and second centuries were house churches according to archaeological evidence; the first remains discovered of a building are from Dura-Europos, northeast of Israel, dated about the year 250 CE.) Consequently the church was not huge, but just how big is hard to tell. From the comments in the letter, one might guess that the number may have been twenty or thirty adults.

The **thesis** of 1 Thessalonians is: **All faithful Christians shall be saved into the Kingdom of God.**

As you read this short letter, note that it is similar to correspondence which we might send. It has a salutation, complimentary comments, progression to more serious matters, answers to the biggest concern, then concluding words and remembrances.

The authors reassure the Thessalonians that Jesus is coming again soon, even though time is passing and he hasn't come yet. Jesus' resurrection is the assurance that he is coming again.

The "I," presumably Paul, reminds the Thessalonians that he worked hard there without pay—he supported himself. From the references by Paul about his self-support, it appears that he was a leather worker. He may have set up a shop near the city market and witnessed to his faith while he plied his trade.

The letter refers to "persecutions," but is not explicit. It was written a dozen years too early for Nero's fire, but it is close to the time when Jews were expelled from Rome for a controversy over a "Crestus," which may, and only may, refer to Christ. It may be that in Thessalonica as well as in Rome and in other cities Jesus Followers were recruited from the ranks of the Jews, but the Jews who remained Jews may have made life difficult for the recruits even to the point of public disturbance. Any such disturbance would have attracted the attention of the local magistrates who would have taken action to keep the peace.

The letter urges the Thessalonians to live morally and to love one another.

Then the big problem is addressed: what is the fate of the believers who have died before the second coming of Jesus? The letter assures the church that those disciples who have died will be resurrected at the coming of Jesus. Not only will they be resurrected, but also Jesus will bring them with him. Then those who have not died will join Jesus and the resurrected disciples "in the air." All will be with the Lord forever in the Kingdom of God.

Exactly when this spectacular "day of the Lord" is coming is a mystery which only God knows, but its soon coming is certain.

The letter closes with greetings and best wishes. The verse 5:27 may be an addition after Paul's letters became important to the church at large. Probably there were more letters he and his mission wrote which are not extant.

1 Corinthians

The occasion for this correspondence with the church in Corinth is morality. Members of the church are behaving immorally—grossly immorally, according to the authors. The letter answers the problem with instructions for Christian living.

There were several letters exchanged between Paul's contingent and the Corinthian church, probably more letters than we have. This letter, called "1 Corinthians," probably was written about 52-54 CE. The salutation states that it is from Paul and Sosthenes.

Corinth was a major port city on the isthmus between the Greek mainland and Peloponnesus. It was about forty miles southwest of Athens. Also, it was the seat of the Roman government for Achaia. The city had a reputation for being on the bawdy side due to behavior of the sailors from many nations who docked there. The city temple in Corinth was dedicated to Aphrodite, the goddess of love. There were many large houses in Corinth which could have held a score or more Christians for their meetings.

The letter is lengthy and has several minor points in addition to the major one about morality. The **thesis** of 1 Corinthians could be multiple, although this single one might be inclusive: **Moral Christians shall enter Jesus' soon-coming Kingdom of God.**

As you read this excellently written letter, note at least these points. Paul and Sosthenes take account of divisions in the church in Corinth because the teachers are inconsistent on their instructions. The authors make quick work of this problem by the overwhelming assertion that none of the teachers were crucified for any of the members; rather Jesus was crucified for them all. Loyalty must be given to Jesus and all instruction must be in accord with his teachings.

The letter acknowledges the "foolishness" of the crucifixion, that is, a savior was not supposed to be crucified, according to the wisdom of the world; but God uses this foolishness of the cross to bring salvation. Jesus, crucified, saves. The letter commands the church to get that point straight!

Several types of immorality are noted involving sex, greed, idol worship, reveling, drunkenness, and robbing. The answer to immorality of these types is to drive out the committers from the church.

Evidently some members are suing other members in court—no charges are named. In any case, the letter directs the members to settle their differences within the church, which is a better place to settle problems than the secular courts. Surely fellow Christians are better judges than pagan magistrates, the letter asserts.

The letter returns to the topic of immorality and states that fornicators, idolaters, adulterers, male prostitutes, sodomites, thieves, and robbers cannot be parts of the body of Christ, that is, the church. Christ's body is pure; therefore, the members of the body on Earth must be pure.

The subject of marriage is raised. Paul gives his opinion that it is better for church members to be single, as he is single, so that they can proclaim the Gospel without the time-consuming hindrances of marriage and family. In fact, if persons are married, it would be better to abstain from sexual intercourse and birthing children because the time is short until the Kingdom is coming and there is the work of proclaiming the Gospel that must be done. Paul makes one concession to those whose passion can't be constrained: go ahead and marry.

The letter examines the status of various categories of people and urges them to stay in their places and serve Christ well since there is not time to make big changes socially when the Kingdom is about to come.

The letter notes that since idols are not real, food offered to them is not contaminated and may be eaten. However, older members are not to eat such food in front of newer members lest the newer members get the impression that the older members approve of idols.

The issue of paying the preacher is treated by simply noting that a laborer is worth his hire; but Paul points out his mission team's generosity in not charging the Corinthians for their labor.

The letter brings up the wearing of head coverings in worship, but gives conflicting answers.

It gives clearer answers on the observance of the Lord's Supper in chapter 11, and on proper behavior at congregational dinners.

The letter treats church order. It gives taxonomy for leadership. Top spot goes to the Apostles, then prophets, teachers, the power elite, healers, assistants, leaders, and finally those who speak in tongues. Evidently some church members who were given the spiritual gift of speaking in tongues were lording it over members who did not receive that gift. The letter reprimands them. Instead of vying over an exotic gift, all members should be seeking the three cardinal Christian virtues: faith, hope, and love.

A short interpolation occurs in 14:33b-36. Church historians note that there was a push in the late first century to exclude women from leadership in the church. Paul did not exclude them. Therefore, it is asserted that this passage is not Pauline, but was added thirty to fifty years later.

The letter returns to the basic Pauline interpretation of the Jesus event. It cites the resurrection of Jesus and his transformation from a material body to a spiritual body. His followers are to seek and are to expect transformation in the Kingdom to spiritual bodies who live forever.

The letter concludes with aphorisms and greetings.

2 Corinthians

2 Corinthians has some of the themes of 1 Corinthians, and adds a few. The letter wanders from problem to problem. The original compilers of 2 Corinthians must have had some order in mind, but it is difficult for us to find it. The letter mentions "afflictions" imposed on the members by non-members, but does not give their specific nature. The authors of the letter seem to have a grievance with the church at Corinth, but do not name the grievance.

This correspondence is a collage of letters put in writing probably by 55 CE. 2 Corinthians is printed in the New Testament as if it is one letter, even though it comprises more than one. As it stands, it mentions that the authors are Paul and Timothy.

An overall **thesis** is problematic, but this one might suffice: **Paul is an authentic apostle of Christ.** While there are specific church problems addressed, the larger concern seems to be with Paul's authority: Is he, or is he not, qualified to advise Christians on their conduct?

Through chapter 7 this book acclaims the superior glory of Christ Jesus in such a way that it appears that Paul and Timothy are trying to convince themselves as well as the Corinthians of this superiority. You might find it helpful and explanatory to list the premises in these chapters that evidence the nature of Jesus.

Chapters 8 and 9 concern the solicitation of funds from Corinth for relief of persons in the drought-stricken areas of Judea. Jesus Followers in Judea, as well as the rest of the population there, are in need. The Corinthians, the authors claim, can afford to be more generous in their donations than other churches of the area. The rationale is that since God sacrificed his son, Corinthians should be willing to make sacrificial offerings.

Paul takes up directly the questioning that some persons in Corinth are making about his apostleship. He reminds them that he has the Lord's commendation. He acknowledges that he may have been weak in his speeches, but he can be harsh in his actions.

In chapter 12 an astral journey is described. Paul seems to be speaking. He has had revelations from God too sacred to be told, but in order to keep him humble the Lord has put a "thorn in his flesh" (the thorn is never specified).

Paul defends his labor among the Corinthians at no pay. He attacks the Johnny-come-lately "super apostles" because they ask for pay.

In closing, the letter reasserts God's power as the source of all blessings, rather than any of Paul's merit. This is very good Jewish theology—to attribute good to the power of God. The letter closes with various greetings.

It may be well to note a condition that affects all of the letters in the Corinthian correspondence. Paul preached in the beginning that the Kingdom of God was imminent, coming soon, within his lifetime. Some believers interpreted that to mean the Kingdom was being actualized immediately as persons repented and were baptized. Therefore, they were in the Kingdom. The Kingdom had come. Where was it? It must be the church.

What was bothersome in all this was that the Kingdom was supposed to be one of pure righteousness. In the churches, however, there was evil behavior. Thus, Paul and his cadre had to change their preaching to "not yet," that is, the Kingdom is imminent, but hasn't come yet. Paul is designated as saying that he compares this "suffering" of evil in the churches to Jesus' suffering. He calls on Christians to expect suffering/imperfection/evil, but to be alert for the coming of the Kingdom in its fullness with the second arrival of Jesus. He personalizes this to himself in a further use of the suffering paradigm, by comparing his own suffering to the suffering of Jesus. He views his suffering as a preparatory event to the coming of the fullness of the Kingdom.

2 Corinthians is a vivid record of the struggles of Paul and his mission team to pioneer their way through territory where no one had gone. Remember that the four Gospels had not been written yet. Remember that the works

of the other New Testament writers had not been composed yet. Remember that every place the mission founded a church was a brand new event. Remember that there were no church manuals or books of discipline to follow. 2 Corinthians reminds us of the heroic treading where no one had trod by Paul's missionary team. This correspondence records their intensive attempts to develop Christianity credible to its Christ.

Galatians

Galatians is the most systematic letter yet to be sent over the signature of Paul. It is a concise exposition of the essential Gospel, according to Paul. Its **thesis** could be stated: **Grace plus faith equals justification.**

The letter to the Galatians carries some uncertainty as to its provenance. This is because Galatia was a territory in Asia Minor, in what is now Turkey, which did not always have well-defined borders. In addition, the records are not certain as to whether Paul went to that area. Furthermore, there are no specific cities or churches named. The letter simply is to the Galatians, that is, to the Jesus Followers in Galatia. There are scholars who conclude that this letter is addressed to the churches just south of Galatia, churches such as Antioch of Psidia, Iconium, Lystra, and Derbe, and that the term "Galatia" is used loosely as an inclusive denominator. It was Paul's strategy to preach the Gospel in major cities, and these cities would meet that criterion.

The letter states that its author is Paul. From hints here and there in the New Testament, it can be assumed that Paul seldom wrote letters in his own long hand, that he had some kind of trouble writing in small letters, and that members of his team served as his scribes. Paul, it is assumed, had the final say as to the wording of the writings, regardless of who did the actual composition, before he signed them. The date of the writing of this letter was probably about 55 CE.

As you read this letter, here are some points to note:

The tone of the letter is caustic. Paul is not pleased with events happening among the Christians in Galatia. The language he uses has been softened somewhat in the English translations.

In chapter 1 Paul claims that he has been given the true Gospel in direct revelation from Christ, implying that his authority is not to be questioned. He gives several details about his activities between the time of the revelation and his missionary journeys.

Chapter 2 describes the Jerusalem Conference held about the year 49 CE which the book of The Acts of the Apostles also describes; the two descriptions are considerably different. Galatians states that the Conference commissioned Peter to work among the Jews, and Paul and Barnabas to work among the Gentiles. Galatians claims that the major outcomes of the Conference were that Paul and his company were approved evangelists to the Gentiles and that they should "remember the poor." (You can compare Galatians 2 with Acts 15.)

The letter of Galatians implies that there are ex-Jews in the churches of Galatia, or perhaps Jewish agitators, who cling to the Law of Moses as a prerequisite to entering the Way of Jesus. Paul emphatically states that the Law does not save; rather Jesus saves. Therefore, becoming Jewish before becoming Christian is unnecessary. If the Law saved, then it would not have been necessary for God to have sent Jesus, nor for Jesus to have died on the cross. Furthermore, it is Jesus who sends the Holy Spirit upon believers, not the Law.

In 3:10 Paul makes it clear that faith/trust in Jesus imputes righteousness. Obedience to the Law could be a post-Christian behavior, but not a pre-Christian requirement. The Law has a different purpose: it is to guide persons in Godly behavior. The Law is not the carrier of salvation.

Paul continues to compare the Law and the Gospel. He transfers the true progeny of Abraham from Abraham's own children to Jesus. Jesus is the true "offspring." Therefore, the continuing true offspring are those who have faith in Christ; or to put it another way consonant with the original language, the continuing true offspring are those who trust in the faith of Christ, the faith that Jesus had in God. Christians are the true heirs of God's Covenant.

Paul asserts that Jesus has abstracted the Law into the Way of the Jesus movement. The gist of this Way is to "love your neighbor as yourself."

Galatians lists the nine fruits of the Holy Spirit, nine behavioral modes that a true offspring manifests, in 5:22:

love, joy, peace, patience, kindness, generosity, faithfulness, gentleness, and self-control.

This letter ends with a triumphant claim that Christians are "new creations" in Christ, and are no longer under the old Law. The benediction is pronounced, praying for the grace of the Lord Jesus the Christ to be with the spirits of the Christians in Galatia. "Amen."

After reading through this extraordinary letter, you probably have noted this about the Law and the Gospel. Paul tries to validate the Jesus movement by showing that it is the fulfillment of the original Hebrew/Jewish religion; but, in doing so, he is aware that the rite of circumcision and indeed the whole of the Law are in that original religion. Therefore, he is driven to repudiate the entire Law including circumcision in order to validate the Jesus event.

This letter demonstrates how Paul does this. Paul does not repudiate the ethical aspects of the Law; indeed, he follows them himself. What he emphasizes is that justification is a divine act not predicated by Jewish Law (or by any law/legalisms of anyone else). Justification is the result of God-initiated grace accepted in faith.

Later correspondence tells us more about the development of Christianity.

Chapter 11

Christianity—
Later Development

Introduction

In this chapter the later correspondence will be treated: Romans, Philippians, Philemon, 2 John, and 3 John. These furnish information on the continuing expansion and development of Christianity.

These books have no singular theme. They consider topics such as church finances, salvation, ethical conduct of those who have been saved, appreciation for hospitality, slavery, the immanence of the Kingdom of God, correct teaching, caring for one another, faithfulness, and true belief. They seek to establish an orthodoxy—their interpretation of the right way of Christian faith and order.

They all address the later members of the church who need spiritual guidance on nearly every aspect of Christianity. These later members have come from the Gentile world. They have varying degrees of acquaintance with Christianity's mother religion, Judaism, which gave Christianity basic theology and ethics. All appear to have some degree of need for education on proper faith and order.

These books were composed approximately 56-150 CE. They treat both local and general conditions in the church. We shall study them in their probable chronological order of composition. Reading each of them in full, at a single sitting, is recommended.

Romans

The letter to the Romans is a stand-alone document, but it includes a lengthy reworking of the theme of justification discussed in Galatians. Romans adds material to Galatians and has a longer challenge to the Christians to live worthily as Christ's church. This book is less caustic than Galatians inasmuch as Paul's apostolic authority is not under question.

Rome was the capital city of the ruling power in the Western world. It had a long history, having been founded in 753/752 BCE. While it had been an important city for centuries, it had been consolidating imperial power only since a hundred years or so before Jesus. By a hundred years after Jesus it had become an empire of unparalleled position in the world. In the time of the writing of the letter to the Romans in the late 50's CE, the city had a population of about a million people. It was not a sprawling city, since walking was the main means of transportation. It did have public works improvements, such as water brought from the hills in sturdy aqueducts, and a sewer system in some parts of town.

When this letter of Romans was written, Nero was the Emperor. The emperor governed under two mandates: one was to govern well using the nearly complete authority of his office; the other was to uphold the constitutional law of Rome. The law was different from the kind of law code of Alexander the Great's empire, and different from common law. It provided for avenues of redress of grievances and for distinct trial procedures for citizens. (The constitutional law pattern of Rome has furnished the pattern for constitutional law in many modern nations, including our own.)

You recall from the book of The Acts of the Apostles that sometime in the mid to late 50's. Paul was arrested in Jerusalem. He did not receive, he believed, fair trials and so appealed, as a Roman citizen constitutionally could do, to the Emperor for a hearing of his case. He was sent to Rome for such a hearing about the year 60, or about two or so years after the writing of this letter. Before his trial in Rome, Paul wrote, or dictated, this correspondence to the church in Rome; the letter has his name alone as the author.

There appear to have been many local churches in Rome. The churches at that time had no corporate buildings. The churches met in the homes of the members. How many "house churches" there were is unknown. How they stayed in touch with each other is unknown. Moreover, how the first one was started there is unknown. Estimates about the number of followers of the Way in Rome in Paul's time vary widely from a few hundred to several thousand. According to The Acts of the Apostles, not a whole lot of members welcomed Paul to the city when he arrived, and not a whole lot kept him company. When all is said and done, the historical records just aren't available for us to describe well the church in Rome or Paul's stay there.

What is known from Paul's letter is that the church in Rome was important, substantial, financially able, and surviving well without his involvement. At the time of writing, Paul had never been to Rome, at least since he had converted to Christianity.

A single **thesis** for Romans is difficult to formulate because of a multiplicity of themes. Perhaps this lengthy thesis will suffice: **Paul's Christian beliefs and conduct are so correct that the church at Rome ought to contribute financial support for his mission to Spain.**

Paul's letter begins with a firm claim that his Christian beliefs are fully orthodox. Evidently Paul thought that he had to state his beliefs clearly, as well as acceptably, to the church at Rome in order to get its approval and support. He presents his theology at length. He uses most of the first eleven chapters to justify his basic stance that right relationship with God brings salvation. This relationship is established between persons and God via faith. Faith in this context means trust.

Two facets of this faith are mentioned, and it is not entirely clear which facet is meant, or if both are meant. The statement in Romans which extols faith asserts that "salvation is to everyone who has faith." What is not entirely clear is whether this means the faith of a Christian, or the faith of Jesus. Scholars debate over the Greek wording as to the exact reference. If it means that Jesus showed a trusting faith in God, then the Christian is saved by Jesus' faith; or if it means that the Christian must show a trusting faith in God and/or Jesus, then the Christian is saved by the Christian's faith. Either seems reasonable, except that the latter smacks of human accomplishment, whereas the larger point Paul is making is that salvation is God's act. Paul reinforces God's primacy by stating in the book that human action, even the full keeping of the Jewish Law, does not save persons. The factor of faith is the key. Trusting faith establishes, or re-establishes the right relationship of persons with God. Thus, salvation lies in right relationship with God.

In another part of this correspondence Paul describes the conduct becoming Christians who have entered the right relationship with God. He states his conviction that Christians are to "present your bodies as a living sacrifice…to God." Paul expresses a similar mystical sense to his statement in 6:4-5 that "we have been buried with him by baptism into his death…united with him in a resurrection like his." A mystical unity with Christ is established, a relationship of such import that Christians are to live as Jesus himself lived, as if they and Jesus are one. Paul implies that he lives this way.

Paul expresses his strong desire to preach the Gospel westward from Rome all the way to Spain. The letter tactfully but pointedly requests the support of the Roman church for his mission.

As you read and study this letter which the fourth century scholars and the Council of Carthage thought was so important that Romans was placed before all the other correspondence, you may benefit from noting these points:

The letter at the beginning declares God's primacy in the process of salvation. God acts in Christ to bring about right relationship. This is verified by God in the resurrection.

Salvation is meant to include all people of every tribe and nation.

God has revealed himself in nature, but some people have disobeyed God by worshipping the creatures of nature rather than the creator; this breaks the relationship with God which God wants all to have. Those who break the relationship deserve to die, to be separated forever from God. A special type of these relationship-breakers, the hypocrites, is especially doomed in Paul's judgment. Paul declares that only Christ redeems persons from the broken relationship. Salvation is available to all who believe in Christ's merit, who trust that Jesus is God's way of doing things. The faith of Jesus satisfies God.

That is exactly why Jesus died, to justify by his blood those who have broken their relationship with the divine. They cannot be saved on their own; they need the additive of Jesus to be saved from the wrath of God. This saved state nullifies the sin of Adam which has been visited on all mankind. This saved state also nullifies individual sins.

The symbol of being saved is baptism, baptism by immersion. This depicts the dying with Christ, being buried with Christ, and being raised with Christ in the new and Kingdom-like life.

Jesus is vital because he frees persons not only from corporate and individual sins but also from the mystical power of sin. Paul describes the mystical power of sin in personal terms, as if there is a spirit/person loose in the world who pushes people to sin. The result of Jesus' action is that the mystical power, this reified sin, is overcome. Persons in faith are free from this mystical power of sin. These persons are now "dead to sin." No mystical power on earth or anywhere else in all creation is strong enough to undo the union between the Christian and the Christ.

In chapter 9 Paul discusses predestination and free will. If God is completely in charge, then does God will sin? Does God will salvation? How does human free will—if there is such—enter into the salvation process? Paul does not answer this problem so much as he talks around it. On the one hand he reaffirms his belief that God has acted with prevenient grace; on the other hand he believes that humans are responsible for responding. Paul claims that this may be inscrutable, but it is true.

Chapter 12 emphasizes the ethics facet of the faith relationship. It includes a section on good, caring, and peaceful behavior. It even counsels full obedience to the state.

The letter draws to a close with further admonitions, wishes of Paul to come to Rome, and personal greetings. An unusual passage at the end is, "I, Tertius…," used as if it is Paul speaking; nowhere else is Paul addressed as "Tertius"; many scholars think that Tertius refers, not to Paul, but to the scribe who penned the book of Romans.

Chapter 16 has been questioned by some scholars as to its authenticity. It does raise a big point of contention: since Paul has never visited the church in Rome, since Paul has been very busy in other parts of a large empire, how could he know so many Christians in Rome? This is especially striking inasmuch as elsewhere it is stated that not many greeted or visited Paul.

A signal point about the entire letter is how frequently Paul wrestles with the nature of salvation. He uses a long list of terms in speaking about salvation: obedience, belief, trust, justification, sacrifice, redemption, reconciliation, union with Christ, predestination, good behavior, obedience to the government, love for neighbor, freedom of life-style, and an indication that salvation will be completed only in the coming Kingdom of God.

The book's final three verses appear to be a benediction that may have been used by churches. It is an eloquent paean of praise that lists major theological topics in this correspondence: mystery, God, faith, and Christ Jesus.

Philippians

The letter of Philippians is a happy, short letter of appreciation from Paul and Timothy to the church in Philippi. The authors had been treated hospitably by the church.

Philippi was a medium size city on the coast north of Thessalonica in Macedonia. The population there was mixed, consisting of immigrants from several parts of the empire in addition to the indigenous population. There was a significant Jewish contingent in the city.

Paul and his colleagues worked there in the early 50's CE and made converts to Christianity. A letter from a Christian bishop, Polycarp of Smyrna, written about 125, states that the church in Philippi was doing well in the second century.

The date of writing of Philippians appears to be the late 50's or very early 60's, say 58-62.

A **thesis** for Philippians is: **Mutual caring prefigures the Kingdom of God.**

As you study this book, these salient features may be of help:

The work begins with a cordial greeting and a statement of appreciation for assistance the Christians in Philippi gave to Paul's mission. Paul expresses a wish to return to Philippi, but until he can do so he will send emissaries from his team.

In 2:5-11 there is a hymn cited. Many scholars view this hymn as having been in use in the Christian movement for some years; the letter quotes the lyrics. It would be interesting if Paul and Timothy had footnoted the source of the hymn. The words are so expressive of the gist of Christian faith that they are being set and reset in music to our day.

The letter encourages the readers to remember several theological points. One is that the righteousness of God is based in faith. Another is that human hope is fulfilled in Christ Jesus. Another is that the second coming of the Lord is "near."

The authors close this correspondence with friendly exhortations, acknowledgements, and greetings.

A benediction is given as a prayer that the grace of Christ will be with the Philippians.

The letter does have a few places where the transitions are abrupt. Some scholars suggest that the letter may have been composed in pieces and that Timothy glued them together on a rainy afternoon. Nevertheless, the letter shows the deep affection Paul and Timothy felt for the church in Philippi, and assumedly, the deep affection that the church felt for them and their mission.

Philemon

The letter to Philemon is addressed to an individual rather than to an entire church.

Philemon is believed to have lived in Colossae. He owns a slave named Onesimus. Apparently the slave has run away, perhaps has taken some of his owner's wealth, but has been converted to Christianity by Paul's mission. The occasion for the letter is what to do now.

Theoretically, in Christ there is no distinction between slave and master; all are one. Paul and Timothy do not urge Philemon to free Onesimus, but they do urge him to treat Onesimus as a Christian brother. The implications of "brother" are bothersome. Should the slave return to the master? If no, then is not the slave "stealing" from his master, and Paul and Timothy are accomplices? If yes, then how are Philemon and Onesimus to treat each other, and in what capacities? What should happen at church? Should they sit next to each other, or one above the other? What if the slave is asked to teach—could a master learn anything from a slave?

This letter carries the names of Paul and Timothy as its authors. From the letter we can know that Paul is in prison—although the prison is not named; if the letter is early, then it could have been written from Ephesus or some other city in that area; if it is late, then it could have been written from Rome. It probably is late and was written about 58-62.

A **thesis** for the letter to Philemon could be: **Slave and master are brothers in Christ.**

The letter tells how Onesimus has become a Jesus Follower and a very helpful worker in Paul's mission.

The letter reminds Philemon that he, too, is a convert of Paul's mission. Consequently, Philemon owes a great debt to the mission for his new life in Christ and his coming life in the Kingdom of God.

The letter calls on both Philemon and Onesimus to be one in Christ. It ends with a few exhortations to be righteous, do good deeds, and work hard. The greetings are very short, as is the benediction.

2 John

The correspondence entitled "The Second Letter of John" is a scanty letter of about three hundred words in English, fewer in Greek. It is addressed to an "elect lady and her children." It is from "The elder."

The attribution of this letter to "John" was done by someone in the late second century who asserted that the Apostle John wrote this letter, as well as 1 John and 3 John. Modern scholarship and philological work have shown that the Apostle John was not the author of any of these. For an Apostle to call himself an "elder" was not done in the records we have; besides, it would have been a demotion to go from Apostle to elder. The identity of the author has not been established. The probable reason that someone attached the name John to the letter is that the letter extols Christian love in a manner similar to The Gospel According to John.

A pertinent **thesis** for this letter is: **Love for one another is the true teaching.**

In the salutation the "elect lady" is mentioned. Who this is has not been determined. If it means a local church, then it is an address found nowhere else in the New Testament. If it means the church at large, than again no other New Testament writer uses the term this way.

Furthermore, "her children" are saluted. Does this refer to actual offspring of a notable woman? Does this refer to members of the church? We are left with considerable uncertainty about this term; hence, uncertainty about the origin and destination of this bit of correspondence.

The content of the letter is the only clue to the date of its writing. Telling items are the references to "many deceivers" and to "antichrists." By the date of writing, the church has had enough time to have had "many" whose teachings have not been true. The church has had time for more than one antichrist (a term meaning anyone who gives false teaching) arise to wrestle members "away from" the more dominant doctrines of the church. In another statement, the letter asserts that some instructors have gone "beyond" the teaching of the dominant church. Evidently enough time has passed that the correct content of Christianity has been formulated, at least formulated in the mind of the author of 2 John; thus, the author can know what "beyond" constitutes. A possible date for the composition of the letter is 100-150, probably closer to 150 than to 100—a date about ninety years after Paul's correspondence.

2 John says that "some" of the elect lady's children are not walking in the truth. It doesn't say that some are.

The letter calls on the children to love one another, which love is shown when the children keep the Lord's commandments. Deceivers and antichrists are the non-lovers.

The author sends greetings from the children of the sister of the elect—again, it doesn't name these. The author expresses his hope to see the recipients in person, soon, and so this short letter should suffice until he comes.

3 John

3 John is a letter which was grouped by the early Christian church with 1 John and 2 John as a trilogy. As we read it, we can see some of their logic in doing so. On the other hand we can see some of their illogic in doing so.

3 John is addressed from an "elder" to "Gaius," who is one of the elder's "children." The author is unknown. The date of composition could be 100-150 CE.

The **thesis** of 3 John is: **Faithfulness to the truth is good.** Truth seems to be the main concern, although hospitality is a topic repeatedly mentioned.

The letter endorses the "friends" of the author who have been received hospitably by Gaius' church. "Friends" can be translated as "brothers," and it may be assumed that the elder means fellow Christians. He notes that the friends refused to accept hospitality from "non-believers," and rightly so. The elder thinks that Christians should be entertained by Christians when they travel away from home, not by non-believers.

The author also calls the friends "my children." Evidently the author is a spiritual father to them. "Elder" could mean "bishop," which would imply that the author is an overseer of a group of house churches.

Farther in the book, the elder charges that Diotrephes is teaching falsely and is spreading false rumors about the elder. Diotrephes is adding insult to injury by preventing members of the church from hosting the elder's friends. The elder enjoins the members of Gaius' church to honor another member, Demetrius who is good, but shun Diotrephes who is evil.

3 John closes with a wish of the author to come soon to see Gaius and his church; thus, he will make the letter short. The last sentence is an instruction to greet the friends, "each by name," although the author lists no names. No comment on the significance of doing so is given.

3 John hardly gets going before it stops.

This later development of the church does not speak specifically about church organization. Further New Testament writings do.

Chapter 12

Christianity—Organization

Introduction

There are three short books in the New Testament which are like manuals for organizing the church. The books are 1 Timothy, Titus, and 2 Timothy. They are written in the form of letters.

At first in the Jesus movement there was no need for church manuals. Jesus was expected to return soon, very soon, and so he would establish standards and direct activities. Paul, the founder of many local churches, did not take time to put a leadership hierarchy in place in those churches. Evidently he thought that all members could share congenially in running an organization until Jesus returned. When year after year went by and Jesus did not return, the egalitarian method of Paul proved insufficient to manage growing numbers of members and churches. Consequently, churches began formulating policies and procedures. By about 100-120 CE these three manuals were written to guide church order. They also are called by some scholars, "Pastoral Epistles."

The topics treated in the manuals could be outlined in several ways. One way is to organize them under three categories: office, creed, and canon.

The office pertains to the leadership. After Jesus is gone, then after his Twelve Disciples/Apostles are gone, who should be in charge? If offices are instituted, what should be the duties and qualifications? How should leaders be selected? What if a church gets so large that it needs more than one host to call it to order? and so on.

The creed pertains to the beliefs. What must a person believe in order to be accepted as a Christian? Is it enough to say, "Jesus?" Is more required, "Jesus is Lord?" Should something about his person be said, "He was born of Mary, lived in Galilee, was…?" Thus, minimal statements of necessary belief in Jesus were formulated.

The canon pertains to the literature. It designates what written works are edifying to the church, so edifying that they are special, sacred, and scriptural. In the early years of the church, the stories about Jesus were passed around verbally—there was no need for written works if the Lord were going to return soon. When Paul began his mission work he found it necessary to write to the churches about various theological and practical problems that they were having. When Jesus did not return by the time Paul died, several authors wrote Gospels to set forth their beliefs and faith-statements. Then additional works appeared on all sorts of facets of faith and order of Christianity. There were many more works written than have been included in the New Testament. The selection of the "proper" works went on nearly to the end of the fourth century before a definitive table of contents of holy writ was made by the dominant variety of Christianity.

The manuals before us are attempts to organize the church properly. These manuals treat the leadership/office, the beliefs/creed, and the literature/canon for the church. They have materials in them that still are followed in church disciplines.

1 Timothy

1 Timothy purports to have been written by Paul to Timothy. At one time there was a Timothy on Paul's mission team. The manual makes it sound as if Timothy has become the local pastor of a church and is looking to Paul for advice. There is no evidence for such an assumption, however. The book more probably is a very, very late first or early second century manual written either by a person with the same name as Paul or is written pseudonymously; and the recipient is either a person with the same name as Timothy or is sent pseudonymously.

The author is not being dishonest or deceitful. The author, quite to the contrary, is genuinely concerned with the faith and order of the church. He writes to instruct Timothy and to improve church life. Neither the place of writing nor the destination of the manual is given.

A **thesis** for 1 Timothy is: **The true church is ordered properly.**

In studying this manual, these items are noticeable:

The letter cautions against false teachers. Evidently there are teachers in the church who are denigrating the Gospel, at least the Gospel as delivered by Paul and Timothy. These false teachers describe the law wrongly by bringing in Gnostic doctrines or by using wild speculation, and the like. The manual reminds the church leader to teach that it is Christ who saves sinners.

There follows a directive to pray for peace, especially for political peace. It may have reference to the recent persecution of Domitian in the 80's and 90's, or to unknown conditions, or even to a daily concern for peace.

A section on women in the church relegates them to being quiet. Eve is named as one who led men astray, so the manual advises to beware of women.

Qualifications are given for the office of elder, aka presbyter/bishop. The requirements are very stringent. It could be speculated by us as to whether or not the church could find anyone who was qualified. One of the give-a-ways as to the dating of this manual is in 3:6. It says that the officers must not be "recent converts"; for the real Paul and Timothy all the converts were recent. No duties are listed, but it is assumed by most commentators that the elders were to give spiritual direction to the church.

Qualifications are given for the office of deacon. No duties are listed. Probably the duties were similar to those of the servers/finance handlers in the mother church at Jerusalem.

The manual returns to the topic of false teaching, denying that asceticism, celibacy, and/or diet are necessary for church members. Especially the item of encouraging marriage shows this manual to be a much later work than those of Paul, who recommended celibacy.

Timothy's duties as a pastor are listed: public reading of the scripture (which scriptures are not specified), exhorting, teaching, and taking care of the elderly and the widows. The manual approves pay for the elders, which would mean that at least some churches have grown substantially enough to be able to pay elders. Also, it calls for the ordination of elders.

The manual ends without the usual greetings. Instead there is another instruction to Timothy to guard the true teachings: let the rich beware and let Timothy be good!

1 Timothy is a much later work than Paul's letters, probably dating 100-120. It shows a hardening of church polity, exclusion of women, encouragement of marriage, and wariness of teachings that have a Gnostic ring to them, among other items. Its purpose is to establish proper order in the Jesus movement which was constantly bringing in new, untrained members. It treats leadership/office, belief/creed, and literature/canon which were growing concerns of the church in the second century.

Titus

The manual entitled "Titus" is much shorter than 1 Timothy, but it has similar material. Titus also has the same form as 1 Timothy, leading some scholars to conclude that the author may have been the same person for both manuals. The biggest difference is that Titus is addressed to Titus, and not to Timothy.

A **thesis** for this manual is: **The true church is ordered properly.** The writer supports this thesis with instances of church organization and members' behavior.

This manual appears to have been written about the same time as 1 Timothy, between 100 and 120 CE. The author is unknown, but claims the name of "Paul." The recipient is unknown, but is addressed as "Titus"; a Titus was a member of Paul's mission team at times.

The book directs Titus to "put in order" the church office and the life-style of the members. The author addresses elders/presbyters/bishops, teachers, older women, younger women, younger men, and slaves in a manner typical of the times: stay in your place; avoid "stupid controversies," "genealogies," and senseless quarrels; and do good deeds.

Titus closes with several greetings and a directive for all members to work productively.

2 Timothy

The third church manual is 2 Timothy. The book has some of the same material as the other two manuals, but differs in several ways. It does not go into detail about the office of the church. It has more personal testimony. It warns extensively about distressing times, false teachings, false teachers, and hypocritical members.

This correspondence is addressed to Timothy and claims to be from Paul. As we have noted for 1 Timothy and Titus, these names do not fit the author and the addressees of the 50's and 60's CE. Instead, the author of the book uses pseudonymous names and treats topics typical of the period 100-120.

The book warns that in the "last days," presumably the days just before the second coming of Christ and the establishment of the Kingdom of God, there will be "distressing" times. It warns that those who try to live a Godly life in Christ will undergo persecution.

The author gives purportedly autobiographical material about his own last days. He is being sacrificed as a libation for others/the church. The time of his departure is at hand, even though the Kingdom of God has not come in his lifetime as he thought it would. He has kept the faith. He expects a crown of righteousness before the Judge. He has longed for the appearance of Jesus again, but is ready to die anyway. He acknowledges that he has been abandoned by most of his colleagues and friends. He laments that at his defense—presumably at court—no one has come to his support. He expresses faith that the Lord will rescue him from every evil. These statements may come directly from the author about his own life; or they may be words passed down about the original Paul as he went on trial in Rome.

A **thesis** for the book is: **A good church leader opposes false teaching and unchristian behavior.**

The book begins by acclaiming Timothy as a solid Christian. He is a third generation Christian (another indication of the later writing of this manual).

The manual condemns immoral people. It is difficult for us to tell whether the immoral are confined to a particular church, to the church at large, or society in general. The letter speaks of "people" who are immoral. This "people" then refers to everyone, both in and out of the church. If there are this many immoral people in the church, and if they are doing so many immoral acts—many more acts named than in Paul's writings—then this is an indication that the church after the turn of the century either was extremely lax in morals or had taken in so many members so fast that it did not have time to train the newcomers in the ways of the Lord.

2 Timothy warns that two of the members of the church, by name Hymenaeus and Philetus, are teaching that the resurrection of Christians already has taken place. This is false, according to the author, and false according to the Apostle Paul a half-century earlier. The danger of believing that the resurrection already has taken place is that the members of the church will assume that the way they are living equals the way life is meant to be in the Kingdom of God. To both Pauls, sinful behavior has no place in the Kingdom; therefore, at least for this reason, the resurrection of persons and their entry into the Kingdom has not taken place.

The manual acknowledges that in a large house—the church has grown—there are many and varied talents. All members who have truly repented will become "special utensils," useful to the Owner of the house.

The author issues a charge to Timothy to imitate the Apostle Paul. Furthermore, Timothy is to study the scriptures until he becomes proficient in his use of them. Which scriptures are meant is not specified; at least it would be the Jewish Bible, which was canonized about the year 90. The Christian New Testament was several hundred years away from having canonical status, but by 120 some Christian writings may have been accorded scriptural status.

In 4:17 the author claims to have been rescued from the "lion's mouth." There is no identification of the lion. If it means from the lions in the Coliseum, then this is a possibility in that the Coliseum was finished about the year 90.

The book draws to a close with a lament. Then it sends greetings to several named persons. It ends finally with a short prayer of blessing.

Summary

In relevant but not neatly ordered manner, the authors of these three manuals set forth their versions of the correct leadership, belief, and literature for the church. They insist that the church be organized with the proper guides/office, the proper views/creed, and the proper scriptures/canon.

These books were written to keep Christianity true, pure, and expanding. As you read them you can see that they may have departed from beginning Christianity and from the norms of the Apostle Paul. Regardless, such manuals were intended to define the orthodox church.

On both sides of these manuals, further New Testament literature exhorts Christians to live faithfully at all costs.

Chapter 13

Christianity—Exhortations

Introduction

There are ten works in the New Testament which could be classified as Exhortations: Hebrews, Colossians, 2 Thessalonians, Ephesians, Revelation, 1 Peter, James, 1 John, Jude, and 2 Peter. They have in common an urgent call to Christians to remain faithful to the Lord no matter what the consequences might be.

The ten were written toward the end of the first century and well into the second century, about 90-150 CE. They were written in Greek, as was the rest of the New Testament. Some of them are very well written. Evidently Christianity had reached into the small literate class of people, as well as into the large illiterate class.

In addition to being alike in the call to faithfulness, the Exhortations also vary in several respects. Hebrews is long at thirteen chapters, and Jude is short at no chapters, only verses. Some are addressed to specific churches and others are addressed to no one in particular. Some mention their authors, others do not; some are pseudonymous.

The dates of their writings are not given in the books. We may conclude that in order for them to have meaning for their readers, the conditions in the Roman Empire at that time must have been threatening to Christians, at least to Christians to whom these Exhortations were sent. The books acknowledge danger for Christians. What those dangers are exactly is not stated. We do know that the Emperor Domitian became crosswise with Christians because they would not acknowledge his divine spirit status. He is known to have punished and even executed Christians in certain localities, although some historians claim that he did not conduct an Empire-wide pogrom. He ruled from 81-96. His successors were more lenient toward Christians; but we do have materials from Roman records that Emperor Trajan recommended quick action against Christians if they broke the *Pax Romana*. That was about the year 110.

Another external threat was community antagonism. Local citizens in some cities became suspicious about what took place in Christian meetings. The Christians conducted the ritual of the Lord's Supper/Holy Communion in closed sessions. Local citizens did pick up on ritual terms of "my body," "my blood," "eat," "drink," and the like, and they heard that Christians called the Lord's Supper their "*Agape*" feast. *Agape* was Greek for "love"; the populace wondered if the Christians were conducting orgies, then eating the flesh and blood of the babies born. Actually, there were several Greek words for "love," and agape had nothing to do with sex, but meant the kind of deep concern attributed to Jesus.

A further external threat was that non-Christians in some places accused Christians of bringing on natural disasters. Since Christians did not worship the traditional gods who controlled the forces of nature, disasters came because the gods were displeased.

In addition to external threats there were internal threats. One was uncertainty about the apocalypse—should Christians hope for a second coming of Jesus, or not? The early belief that Jesus would come again, soon, was getting continued support on the one hand, but rising doubt on the other hand. This condition caused controversy and disagreement in the "body of Christ," which ideally should be one in doctrine. Various rationalizations were offered by those who refused to give up the belief in a second coming. One was that it was a figurative term which referred to the baptism by immersion of converts inasmuch as they were buried, dead, and then raised to union with Christ.; thus, they said, the messianic age has come—the second coming has come--for anyone who is baptized. Another rationalization was that those upon whom the Holy Spirit has come are collectively the Kingdom of God on Earth; the coming of the Holy Spirit in this way constituted the second coming, the messianic age. Another rationalization was that the church is what Jesus meant when he talked about the Kingdom of God on Earth; thus the church constitutes the second coming, the coming of the messianic age.

Other internal threats were the immorality of some members, false teachings, arrogant leaders, poor leaders, and the rapid influx of Gentiles who had no background in the mother religion of Christianity—Judaism. The Judaizers insisted that Jesus Followers must obey all the Law of Judaism since Jesus and the Apostles were law-abiding Jews. The Gnostics presented a variety of beliefs about the physical reality of Jesus—surely God could not become common flesh and die. What should a Christian believe? In what kind of behavior should basic faith in Jesus issue?

The ten works of Exhortations taken as a whole deal in some measure with external and internal threats. Even though they may not have logical answers or consistent remedies to these threats, all of them have in common the exhortation to remain faithful to Christ. Being faithful to Christ would assure persons a place in the messianic Kingdom of God no matter what external consequences they had to bear. Being faithful to Christ would assure persons a place in the body of Christ on Earth, the church, no matter what disparate opinions might be advanced.

Hebrews

The book of Hebrews may be the earliest of the Exhortations. It is an anachronism. It appears in the New Testament sort of like a bolt out of the blue. It is suddenly there. It claims no author. It is addressed to no one. There are no salutations. The title word, "Hebrews," is not appropriate to the contents. Possibly one of the reasons this book was included by those who gathered the New Testament in the fourth century was that popular opinion at that time credited the Apostle Paul with the authorship of Hebrews. Scholarship now has shown that the Apostle could not have been the author of this work. The date of writing probably was just before the turn of the first century, say 90-95 CE.

Of all genres, Hebrews is considerably like a sermon that an elder, presbyter, or bishop might have preached on any given Sunday. It exhorts the listeners to stand firm for the Christian faith in the face of adversity. Evidently the listeners or readers had experienced persecution or prosecution for following the Christian Way. Such adversities could have included confiscation of property, enslavement, and even execution of fellow Christians.

Hebrews quite probably was delivered not to Hebrews (Jews), but to Gentiles. The content sets forth theology that already would have been known to Jews, but on which Gentiles would need to be informed. The author goes to great lengths to convince the hearers or readers that Christianity is superior to Judaism. His having to say this implies that Judaism is a possible draw for church members; why it is, is not made clear. Could it be that since the Roman rulers had exempted Jews from emperor worship, these church members, because they suffer, are tempted to turn to Judaism and safety? In many ways Judaism and Christianity are similar, but the event of Jesus makes them different, according to Hebrews. Gentiles need to know this in order to be retained in the Christian Way.

A **thesis** for the book is: **Follow Jesus the superior messiah.**

Hebrews begins by asserting that God has spoken through his Son who is superior to the angels.

It continues by noting that Jesus is worthy of the title "Lord" because of his suffering which was a sacrifice to bring about atonement with God. He is the superior sacrifice.

Furthermore, Jesus is the "apostle" and "high priest" of the "confession" of Christians. He is superior to all others.

Jesus does not negate Moses, but he gives further and finer interpretation to Mosaic Law. He is superior to Moses.

Hebrews states that when Christians fail to hold fast to the superior Jesus, then they are being disobedient to God and are immature.

No doubt Christians who know the Lord's teaching to forgive as many as seventy times seven are taken aback by the preacher of Hebrews declaring that Christians have zero times of forgiveness if they fall away from the faith.

The work continues by claiming the superiority of Jesus as Messiah. He is the eternal high priest. He is the Messiah of the line of Melchizedek—the priest of God who preceded Abraham. Jesus does not negate Melchizedek, but he is superior to Melchizedek.

Any and all previous messianic figures were mere shadows of the Jesus to come. In words reminiscent of Plato's "Allegory of the Cave" the Hebrews preacher declares that Jesus is the "really" real Messiah, not a shadow.

The author portrays Jesus in a further, unusually superior manner: Jesus is the New Covenant itself, the Covenant described by the prophet Jeremiah (Jer. 31).

This Exhortation closes with the call to resist all adversaries even if it means death. Those who endure the trials of persecution or prosecution will receive the imperishable Kingdom of God.

The author brings the hearers or readers back to the Jewish base in order to connect them to God's eternal activities, but he does not let them stay there. He returns them to Jewish theology, but not to Jewish practice. He claims that Jesus is the superior Christ, the epitome of all practice and religion.

Colossians

The book of Colossians continues the Exhortations to Christians. It is addressed to the saints, brothers, and sisters in Colossae.

Colossae was an unusual site for Paul's mission group to found a church: his mission usually went to populous cities, not to small ones. Nevertheless, this small city in Asia Minor (now Turkey) near the coast is the site of one of the Paul-founded churches. Colossae might be considered a suburb of Laodicea, the major trade center in the area. At least one Phrygian cult met there, as well as a Jewish synagogue.

The book is brief. Its **thesis** is: **Follow not false teaching.**

Colossians carries the names of Paul and Timothy in the salutation as the authors. These appear to be pseudonyms, however, since the writing was probably 90-100 CE, about forty or fifty years after the first Pauline letter of 1 Thessalonians and about twenty-five or thirty-five years after Paul's death. Timothy himself may have been young enough to have written this exhortation, but there is no outside evidence for this. The issues which this Exhortation treats arose late in the first century.

Colossians begins by declaring that Paul preached to them the "mystery" that has been hidden through the ages. This is a contradiction to the original Paul who didn't make the Gospel mysterious; he thought the Gospel was explicit.

The work calls on the Colossians to beware of the false teachings of "philosophy" and "human traditions." Also, Christians are not to study about the "elemental spirits" of the universe nor yield to "human ways" of thinking. They are not to practice asceticism because it is merely "self-imposed piety." If members of the church submit to human regulations then it shows that they have not been raised with Christ.

Colossians reminds the Christians that they are "hidden with Christ in God." They are to live by the things above, not by the things below. The book lists a number of qualities from above, among them compassion, kindness, humility, meekness, patience, forgiveness, love, and peace.

Colossians mentions modes of worship: singing of psalms, hymns, and spiritual songs to God.

Colossians gives admonitions to wives, husbands, children, slaves, and masters. The wives are to obey the husbands, the children to obey the parents, and the slaves to obey the masters.

The greetings at the end mention Onesimus, someone with the same name as the slave named in the book of Philemon. Also a Mark is named as one of the author's party, although Paul soon rid himself of Mark's presence on his mission journeys. Luke, the "beloved physician" and others are mentioned.

The concluding admonition from the authors is that this book is to be read in a circular manner among the (house) churches.

In summary, Colossians exhorts the readers to abhor various philosophical speculations, human traditions, and celestial elements; and to pray for the authors that they may declare the mysteries of Christ—themes that were being introduced in the churches in the very late first century. The Christians at Colossae must not follow these false teachings because they lead to base behavior and specious theology.

2 Thessalonians

The Exhortations book of 2 Thessalonians follows the book entitled 1 Thessalonians, but it is not a complementary work. This work may have gained a place in the New Testament just for the reason that it sounds somewhat like the first book. It has, however, enough differences to place it at a much later date and by an author other than Paul or his mission team.

Thessalonica was a medum size city of that time. It was the capital of the Roman province of Macedonia. It was a prosperous city with a variety of religions. It was a typical place for Paul and his mission to found a church. They did start a church there in the late 40's CE.

The church, according to 1 Thessalonians, had a problem understanding when Jesus would come again and when the Kingdom of God on Earth would be established. That problem was answered in the first letter. The authors assured the church that Jesus was coming again soon, very soon, and that if any of the members died before the coming, they would be raised with Christ and taken into the Kingdom.

Furthermore, they declared that the time of the second coming was not revealed to them; therefore, the church should be alert for its coming at a moment's notice. 2 Thessalonians differs significantly at this point. It exhorts the church to look for signs of the coming of the Kingdom, and then it would know for sure the time of the Kingdom's coming.

The date of writing of 2 Thessalonians could be anywhere between 90 and 120 CE.

A **thesis** for the work is: **Be faithful in spite of ill fortune.** There may be prices to pay for being faithful, such as persecutions and lawless treatment, but the prices are meager compared to the greater reward for faithfulness. The faithful will participate in the Kingdom as soon as it comes.

Chapter 1 sends comfort to Christians who suffer ill fortune by assuring them that God will avenge those who are persecuting them.

Chapter 2 exhorts church members to stand firm for the faith, no matter what the consequences. Any ills cannot compare to the benefits of the Kingdom.

Chapter 3 nixes free-loading while waiting for the coming of the Kingdom. Evidently some members were lounging around eating others' pot luck dinners while contributing nothing except the excuse that they had to keep free from laboring in order to stay on watch for the soon coming of the Kingdom.

This book is short but pointed. It exhorts Christians to be faithful in spite of persecution and lawlessness. The faithful shall be rewarded.

Ephesians

The book of Ephesians is an Exhortation to the church to behave according to its intended destiny of uniting with Christ. The book bypasses talk about a coming Kingdom of God. It reads as if the Kingdom and the Christian movement are actualized as one and the same.

Ephesus was a major city on the coast of Asia Minor (Turkey). It did not front on the water, but was back a short hike. It had a finely paved road of cut stone down to the water. The public buildings of the city were constructed with white marble, which made Ephesus distinctive and highly visible. One of the buildings was a two-acre-large temple to Diana/Artemis—a huge size for a Greek/Roman temple. Another structure was the stadium which seated fifty-five thousand. The city was the seat of the government of Rome for the area.

Ephesus had a strong Christian church. It was stable, financially able, and the home church of several noted leaders.

For all of this, the book entitled "Ephesians" may or may not have been sent to Ephesus. The oldest manuscripts do not name any destination. The versions we now have name Ephesus as the intended audience. What we can conclude is that the book is an Exhortation to Christians wherever internal controversy over the nature of the Kingdom of God is alienating members one from another.

The claim in the salutation that Paul wrote this book is suspect. Both the vocabulary and the theology are typical of years beyond the Apostle. Probably this letter was written not earlier than 90 CE and not later than 130 by an unknown author.

One thing that can be said with certainty about Ephesians is that it is an excellent literary piece. It was written in Greek, a language which is rich in precise word meaning. It follows a theme from the beginning to the end. It introduces many eloquent words and phrases to Christian thought which carry original and deep meaning. It takes the theology of the Christian movement to levels not heard elsewhere.

The **thesis** of the book is**: Be one Body of Christ.**

In the first chapter the book makes the claim that Christians have been redeemed by Christ. As they are redeemed they are incorporated into a body of believers who constitute, allegorically, the body of Christ on Earth. Christ is the head of that body, and the members are the rest of the parts. Ephesians insists that all members are equally members, even though members in a body have different functions. Jews and Gentiles are one in the body. The one body is here, now—not in the future as the Apostle Paul and earlier followers of the Way believed. Christians are already raised up and are seated with Christ in the heavenly places (remember Paul spoke against the "already raised up" idea).

Chapter 2 has novel phrases, such as "…no longer strangers and sojourners," "…citizens with the saints," "…members of the household of God," "…a holy temple in the Lord," and "…a dwelling place for God."

Chapter 3 proceeds with biographical material about the Apostle Paul, apparently in an effort to give this book more authority. Ephesians has a stopping place at the end of chapter 3. It gives a benediction and an "Amen."

Chapter 4 continues with ethical directions that seem to be part of another correspondence. The Ephesians are told not to live as Gentiles live. This is puzzling. The Apostle Paul was the emissary to the Gentiles. True, he made some converts among the Jews early in his missions, but he soon turned his evangelistic work to the Gentiles. Thus, the Christians at Ephesus are largely, if not completely, Gentiles. Does the author mean not to live as unsaved Gentiles? Does he mean not to live as saved Gentiles? More puzzling, what could it mean for Gentiles who are Gentiles not to live as Gentiles? In any case, all members are to live as if they are part of the body of Christ.

In chapter 5 the author reverts to sacrificial talk by calling Christ a "fragrant offering" and a "sacrifice to God."

This sounds Jewish, but may be a slip because the author is far from being Jewish in theology.

The book continues in chapters 5 and 6 with exhortations to Christians to live righteously no matter what the pressures from within and without are. Ephesians gives directions for family life, children, parents, slaves, and masters. These directions resemble Roman cultural standards more than the new interpretations of ethics that Jesus and Paul gave.

The exhortative thrust of the book is driven home in 6:10-20. Ephesians compares the life of a Christian to that of a warrior who must put on armor in order to survive attacks. The armor is not made of metal, however, but of the virtues of God. This kind of armor can withstand the "wiles of the devil," "rulers," "authorities," "cosmic powers," and "spiritual forces of evil." This kind of armor consists of truth, righteousness, peace, faith, salvation, and the word of God.

Evidently both Earthly powers and cosmic powers are threatening the church. Ephesians makes an eloquent plea for Christians to stand and fight evil. Herein evil is depicted as a suprahuman power, not a human error. The book exhorts: Never surrender to evil! Christians can stand because they are now part of the body of Christ, united with divinity, empowered by God—if they hold fast to the faith.

The book closes with the assurance that Christians can withstand all evil, can live circumspectly, and shall triumph finally if they are one in the one body of Christ.

Revelation

The book of Revelation is an Exhortation in the form of an apocalypse.

An apocalypse is a genre of literature which has a long history. In the Hebrew/Jewish Bible (Old Testament) the book of Daniel is in apocalyptic form. In the Deuterocanon, works which were not included universally in either Testament but which were worthy of study, there are the Apocalypse of Abraham and the Apocalypse of Elijah. In the New Testament, Mark 13 is a mini-apocalypse. The peak time of apocalyptic literature was from about 250 BCE to 250 CE.

The book of Revelation appears to have been written near the middle of this period, about 95 CE. All apocalyptic literature expressed hope for salvation from an evil world or evil circumstances and salvation to a righteous world of divine rule. It exhorted readers to be faithful to God and they would be blessed.

Revelation acknowledges that humans are having difficulty in establishing a righteous world, or as the literature would say, a Kingdom of God. The book returns to the very early Christian hope that God would intervene in history to establish the Kingdom. Revelation expresses full confidence that the cataclysmic intervention of God is sure to come—soon. In the meantime, Christians are to be faithful if they want to be included in the Kingdom.

The book of Revelation is a unique work. Its placement at the end of the New Testament is understandable: those who canonized the New Testament may not have known what else to do with it!

Revelation refers to places and events; but it does so in a peculiar way. It refers to past events as if they are future events. This has been a blessing and a bane. It was, no doubt, a blessing to those who read it in the time when it was written. The book gave them hope in the midst of tribulations. It has been a bane to twenty centuries of those Christians who have interpreted the events referred to in the book as portents of events to come in the twenty centuries that have followed; in so doing they have ignored the meaning for the original readers to whom the book is addressed. Thus far, all predictions about endings of this world by later readers have been mistaken. Moreover, even the writer of the book of Revelation was mistaken about the proximity of an end time.

A **thesis** for the book is: **Be faithful in spite of tribulations.**

At the time of writing, about 95, the Christians addressed by the book were beset with tribulations. One of the tribulations was political in nature. The Emperor Nero had initiated temporary prosecution of Christians in the 60's as scapegoats for the great fire (that he is said to have started) that burned much of Rome. He may have selected them specifically because they did not worship the traditional gods or give expected homage to the Emperor.

There may have been sporadic imperial or local governmental persecutions of Christians in the years immediately following Nero; the records are not extant to say one way or the other. What is more certain is that in the 80's and 90's Emperor Domitian (r. 81-96) prosecuted Christians both in and out of Rome in an imperial manner. It is said that he ordered the confiscation of property, enslaving of believers, and/or execution of church leaders. Domitian did so because of the growing belief that Christians were atheists: they refused to acknowledge the traditional gods; they declared that their God was the only God; and they would not acknowledge the lordship of the divine spirit of the Emperor (the emperors were thought to rule by a kind of divine right and divine spirit). Domitian probably didn't think of himself as immortal or divine, but he thought that the Emperor should be given divine honors in order to maintain the unity of the Roman Empire. When Christians refused to honor him thusly, for theological reasons, he accused them of sedition and allowed his magistrates to prosecute them. The historical record is not clear as to how vigorously Domitian punished Christians, but from the comments in Revelation there is hope in the Christian community that he and others like him will be deposed or eliminated—soon.

Revelation was written toward the end of Domitian's rule. It was written to encourage Christians to stand fast in their faith even if it meant they would be treated violently. The book does not name Domitian, but it refers to Nero as representative of Roman rule—Nero was dead and it was safer to refer to him rather than to a reigning emperor. Furthermore, the book refers to an antichrist who would lead evil forces against Christians and God. A novel but widely believed rumor at that time was that Nero would be resurrected and would return to Earth as the antichrist.

Another tribulation was placed on Christians by the non-Christian population in general. Christians were blamed for natural disasters, disease, and other misfortunes because they did not worship the gods who controlled human fortunes.

Another tribulation was what outsiders thought about Christian meetings. Christians probably had some open meetings for prospective members, but they themselves met in secret or closed sessions. Christians in some locales met before work at dawn or after work at night. Christians met on Sundays and did no work on that day, while non-Christians worked seven days a week.

The suspicion of what Christians did in their closed sessions was the most bothersome. Non-Christians began hearing that the Lord's Supper was a regularly observed ritual in the closed session. In that ritual the Christians "ate the body" and "drank the blood" in memory of Jesus. Couple this with the name Christians used for their meetings, "agape (Greek for "love") feasts," and imaginations went wild. While "agape" did not mean sexual love, rather a Christ-like love for one another, that didn't deter the imaginations of the general populace. Christians were charged with having sexual orgies at night, birthing babies whom they killed, then eating their bodies and drinking their blood. Non-Christians abhorred Christians as the vilest of human beings, beasts even.

Another tribulation was when families were split by one or more members becoming Christian, while the rest remained true to their religion.

Another tribulation was within the church. Paul had founded charismatic churches, that is, churches which were inspired by the Holy Spirit to do right. He expected the cataclysmic, soon coming of the Kingdom of God; hence no permanent order or offices were needed. Church members were to have faith in Jesus, love one another, and behave themselves. The years passed and the Kingdom did not come. More and more Gentile members were added who did not have Jewish morality or Pauline idealism as a base; or they were just too rascally to behave properly.

All these, and perhaps other tribulations, caused the writer of Revelation to renew the cry to God for the Kingdom to come—soon!

As to the book itself, it is fascinating reading. There are accounts of dreams, descriptions of astral journeys, and visions of beasts. The imagery is more in our realm of science fiction, rather than in our realm of real life. Some of the forces are personified in animals who think or act or talk in human ways. Much of the narrative is carried by angels. Most of the book has allegorical rather than historical meaning.

Our tasks are to draw historical inferences from it and to extract its meaning.

The sincerity of the author is not to be doubted. The author longs for salvation from tribulation and salvation to better existence. The author believes that God's justice is retributive, that good will be rewarded and evil will be punished; but the days are dragging on and God's justice has not come. Nevertheless, the author believes that conditions are so bad that God undoubtedly will intervene—soon. Thus he exhorts Christians to be faithful in spite of tribulations.

The book says that the author was "John." No specific John is given. Early Christians jumped to the conclusion that the Apostle John wrote the book. Scholars have found that this is not at all likely. The Apostle John was characterized elsewhere in the New Testament as illiterate. Also, the Apostle would have been about a hundred years old at the time of writing. The same early Christians jumped to the conclusion that the Apostle John also wrote The Gospel According to John. Philologists have found that there is such a huge difference in the linguistic quality of these two books that the same author could not have penned both of them. The Gospel is smooth, fluent Greek; Revelation is rough, uneven Greek. The Christian Bishop Dionysius of Alexandria about the year 250 CE is recorded in Eusibius' Ecclesiastical History as calling the language in Revelation "barbaric."

One way to extract the meaning of Revelation is to examine the factor of hope in it. In common conversation, "hope" is used to denote a wish. In Revelation, "hope" is used to denote a fact. This means that, in the words of the first sermon of the church as delivered by Peter, God has vindicated Jesus as the hope of the world. It means that Jesus has triumphed over evil, all evil, all sin, even death; Jesus has—past tense—done so. The hope in Revelation is expressed not as a wish, but as a fact. God has declared that the end of all has been determined: good shall triumph. The Kingdom shall come. Christ Jesus shall reign. The faithful shall be saved. The kingdoms of this world shall become the Kingdom of Heaven. This is how history shall turn out.

As you can see, this hope may seem every bit as fanciful as four living creatures full of eyes in front and behind, as described in Revelation. The readers, however, are not to get stuck on the fantastic beasts, or on the horses, or on the seal, or on whatever; and, apparently, they aren't. They are looking beyond the figures to the end result: Christ is the accomplished, factual, final hope. Revelation assures Christians that God has acted in Jesus already, and that it is only a matter of a short time until God shall strike his triumphant cataclysmic blow against all adversaries and all evil. Therefore, Christians ought to be faithful in spite of tribulations.

The book begins with its own genealogy: revelation from God to Jesus to an angel to John on the Island of Patmos. John critiques seven churches in Asia Minor.

Then the author is transported to the throne room of God. There amid the splendor of jewels sit twenty-four elders;

in front of them is the crystal sea. Around the throne are a lion, an ox, a human face, and a flying eagle, each with six wings and eyes all around and inside.

The one seated on the throne holds a scroll. On the scroll are seven seals. No one is able to open them except Jesus. Bowls of incense which are the prayers of the saints are given to Jesus the Lamb. Myriad creatures throughout heaven sing praises to the Lamb.

The Lamb opens the seals: a white horse, a red horse, a black horse, and a pale green horse. Each of these is accompanied by many signs and accoutrements. The fifth seal is opened to the souls of those martyred for the Christian cause. The sixth seal is opened to horrendous devastation to the Earth.

Nevertheless, the Earth stands. Four angels hold back further destruction so that one hundred, forty-four thousand chosen ones, twelve thousand from each of the twelve tribes of Israel, can be honored. Countless others from every nation join them and sing praises to God and the Lamb. They are robed in white, signifying that they have been washed clean by the blood of the Lamb.

The seventh seal is opened. It reveals seven angels with seven trumpets. The first angel blows a trumpet and a third of the Earth is burned to a crisp. The second angel blows a trumpet and a third of the maritime part of the Earth is destroyed. The third blows and turns a third of the drinking water of Earth to wormwood. The fourth darkens a third of the sun, moon, and stars. The fifth opens the shaft to the bottomless pit ruled by Abaddon/Apollyon from which come scorpions to sting for five months the people who are not sealed by God (the description of these scorpions is so bizarre that you must read it yourself in 9:7-11).

The sixth angel blows a trumpet and a third of Earth's population is killed by two hundred million troops of cavalry.

A mighty angel comes with a little scroll. He brings a secret message, but when John starts to write it down, the angel stops him. John is commanded to eat the scroll: it is sweet to his taste, but upsets his stomach. John is told to prophesy, but the prophecy is not given here. Various minor disasters follow.

The seventh angel blows the trumpet and God's Temple is opened. The Ark of the Covenant is seen inside.

Then a great portent appears in heaven—a pregnant woman ready to deliver. Another portent appears—a great red dragon with seven crowns. The dragon snatches the baby boy that the woman bears and takes it to God's throne; but the woman flees into the wilderness where God sustains her.

Michael and his angels make war on the dragon. The dragon, aka Devil/Satan, is thrown down to Earth and pursues the woman in the wilderness. The woman is miraculously saved from the dragon. The dragon sulks away to make war on the followers of Jesus.

A beast rises out of the sea. The whole population of Earth worships the beast and the dragon. The beast and dragon slaughter everyone except those whose names are written from the foundation of the world in the Lamb's book of life.

A second beast arises from Earth. Its number, calculated from the numerical equivalents of the alphabet, is 666, very probably a reference to the Emperor Nero and by inference to any adversarial Roman Emperor.

John then sees the Lamb standing on Mount Zion in Jerusalem. There one hundred, forty-four thousand virgins sing a new song to the Lamb and God.

Another angel flies through mid-Heaven and shouts that the hour of God's judgment is come. A second angel announces the fall of Babylon (Rome). A third angel proclaims judgment on those who worship the beast.

A fourth angel urges one like the Son of Man to reap the Earth with a sharp sickle. A fifth angel, and a sixth command the one with the sickle to exercise the wrath of God; and the shed blood flows as high as a horse's bridle for two hundred miles.

Seven new angels appear with seven new plagues. Six pour their plagues on Earth: painful sores, blood in the sea, blood in the fresh water, sun that scorches the disobedient, agony, and drying up of the river Euphrates.

Three foul spirits arrive who assemble the kings of the world for battle at Harmagedon.

The seventh angel cries that the time is come and sends hundred pound hailstones hurtling down from Heaven on the people.

A great whore is introduced as "Babylon the Great," the mother of whores and Earth's abominations. The great whore is drunk with the blood of Jesus Followers. The whore is seated on seven hills (Rome), which also represent seven rulers (Roman Emperors). After a series of interchanges, the woman is doomed to burn up with fire.

Another angel announces in several hymns the destruction of those who oppose God. The Heavenly hosts rejoice in a series of songs.

Heaven opens to a white horse with a rider named Faithful and True, Word of God, King of kings, and Lord of lords. The rider brandishes a sword from his mouth and defeats the beast and its forces in a mighty battle.

John repeats himself with another angel who descends into the bottomless pit. The angel binds the Devil/Satan for one thousand years.

Then John sees three judges on thrones. He also sees the souls of those who have been beheaded for their resolute faithfulness to Jesus and the word of God. They come to life and reign with Christ for one thousand years. This is the first resurrection.

After one thousand years Satan is released and tries to deceive the nations, but fire from heaven consumes Satan; then judgment day comes. The books of records on humans are opened and all humans are judged.

A new Heaven and a new Earth come. A new holy city, Jerusalem, comes. Those who cannot enter it are consigned to the second death—the permanent one.

John is taken on another astral journey to see the New Jerusalem descend. The city has rare jewels. It has twelve gates for the twelve tribes of Israel. It has foundations on which are written the names of the twelve Apostles. It has "pearly gates." There is no Temple here because God and the Lamb are the Temple. They shine ceaselessly so that there is never darkness.

John is then shown the river that "flows by the throne of God." Beside it is the tree of life that bears twelve kinds of fruit. The leaves furnish "healing for the nations." John is reassured by the Lamb himself that he is coming back to Earth—soon.

John feels compulsion to worship. The nearest being is an angel, who refuses John's offered adoration and directs John to worship God.

The Lamb speaks again, saying that he is the "Alpha and the Omega" (the first and last letters of the Greek alphabet), the beginning and the end. The Lamb reassures John that the messages given to him for the seven churches (at the beginning of the book of Revelation) are authentic.

Revelation ends with a warning to editors, scholars, and anyone else: if anyone adds or takes away from the words of Revelation they will have God to pay. Again Jesus asserts that he is coming again—soon. John is exuberant: "Amen. Come!"

This book ends so triumphantly that a student of it is tempted to forget studying it and merely add, "Amen!"

What can be said about Revelation in summary are these points:

1. Context.

An apocalyptic Exhortation such as Revelation is written in an age when times are tough; there is no audience when times are good. As far as we can tell, Revelation was written late in the first century, during or just following the reign of Emperor Domitian who well may have authorized persecutions. When property, family, and life are being taken by force, then Heaven is the only place to turn. The human spirit craves some safe place to reside, and in times of extremity, the safe place is the other world.

Revelation was written for the readers in that tough time of the late first century. It was written to the seven churches and the Christians who were suffering for their faith. The book was written to draw meaning out of the chaos of its own time, not for a subsequent age, not even ours. True, its general point is well taken that in troubled times there is hope in God. The specifics of the visions of Revelation, however, were meant for the suffering and/or wavering Christians then and there.

2. Second Coming.

The very idea of the second coming of Jesus has, by 95 CE, a sixty-five year history. Earlier Paul had expected Jesus to return and construct the Kingdom of God during his lifetime. In the writings of Luke-Acts, thirty or forty years after Paul's earliest letter, Luke acknowledges that the Kingdom is not coming in Paul's lifetime, nor in his lifetime—at least it hasn't. In the Gospel According to John, there is little mention of the Kingdom coming at all; rather, John rationalizes that since the Kingdom didn't come, the interpretation of what the Kingdom is must have been mistaken. John interprets the Kingdom to mean that it is here and now for "whoever believes" in Jesus; it has begun for a believer and continues eternally. In contrast, Revelation reverts to the early belief that a physical Kingdom is coming—soon. It will be God's cataclysmic and final insertion into human history.

3. Allegory.

The signs, numbers, and figures in Revelation have a high degree of allegory. In our time, they would merit the term "fantastic." The examples of this are countless. One such passage describes the eradication of the world and history, but follows immediately with narrative that presumes the world and history are intact. Elsewhere in the book the behavior of the four "this's" and the seven "that's" are incredible.

4. The Beast.

There are references in the middle chapters of the book to Babylon, the beast, and 666. This is veiled talk about Roman rulers meant to inform Christians about the rulers and yet not incite the rulers to further prosecutions.

Evidently the author of Revelation thought that he had to write in veiled terms. Probably this wasn't necessary inasmuch as it was not likely that the Emperor's magistrates would spend their time perusing Christian writings. Recall that the Christian movement by the turn of the first century was quite small in numbers. It claimed only a tiny percentage of the population. Even if there was persecution of Christians by Emperor Domitian, it would have been a minuscule event in the overall history of Rome at that time, although it would have been a gigantic event for persecuted individuals. Nevertheless, the writer takes no chances on public disclosure and writes in double talk.

5. Rationale.

The reason why the book of Revelation is in the New Testament at all has been widely debated. Some becauses can be advanced. One because is that there was actually persecution of some Christians in some places; life and limb for some were in jeopardy.

Another because is that the Christian population was small enough that any decimation anywhere was a newsworthy event for all the rest of the Christians.

Another because is that Roman rule was hated all the more since the Romans conquered Jerusalem and destroyed the Temple in 70 CE, and castigation such as Revelation pours on the Romans would be some consolation to readers who were not practicing Jews but who had roots in Jewish history.

Another because is the expectation of the second coming of Jesus to establish the Kingdom which he didn't succeed in establishing the first time around.

Another because is that an ideal world seems to be an immortal yearning.

1 Peter

The Exhortation entitled 1 Peter is a late first or early second century work from "Peter an apostle of Jesus Christ," to the "Dispersion in Pontus, Galatia, Cappadocia, Asia, and Bithynia."

This is a remarkable salutation. Note first the attributed author. The book does not claim that the author is that Peter who was one of Jesus' Twelve Disciples; and this is rightly so because the book was written decades after the death of that Peter. In chapter 5 the author calls himself "elder," a title that Peter would not use. Actually, the name "Peter" ("Rocky" would be similar in our day) was a common name in that era; the designation "apostle" was used by some in that era even though they were not of the Twelve; and "elder" was a common term for spiritual leaders in the church. A passage elsewhere in the New Testament states that the original Apostle Peter was illiterate; this letter is written not even in the language Peter daily spoke—Aramaic—but in Greek, in excellent Greek. The conclusion is that the author of 1 Peter is either another Peter or is using the name pseudonymously.

Another supposition about the author for which there is no historical substantiation is that perhaps the original Apostle Peter did evangelistic work in Asia Minor/Asia, and this letter is a follow-up to that work; but this goes against other traditions that the Apostle Peter preached mainly to Jews and in the western part of the Empire.

Note second the addressees. The territory to which the letter is addressed is huge. In a time when there were no means of duplicating material except by hand and that by the tiny percentage of people actually able to write, and by the even tinier percentage who were Christian, too, the expectation that this exhortation would be read by all of Asia Minor and/or Asia is very presumptive. Specifically the book is addressed to "Dispersion" Christians. Dispersion referred to Jews who lived outside of Palestine; this letter indicates that some of them had become Jesus Followers. There is some question, however, as to how wide an audience this would be. Other historical material indicates that while many of the first Jesus Followers were Jewish, not many later Christians were; Paul soon took his message to the Gentiles almost exclusively.

In all, 1 Peter has the definite appearance of having been written pseudonymously to someone or some church in Asia/Asia Minor. We can speculate that rather than addressing pressing problems in some single struggling church the author is writing an exhortation to whomever it may concern in the Dispersion. Whether or not anyone specifically reads this work does not seem important to the author; quite possibly he is putting into writing his own felt need without any necessity that his work be read by all or anyone. The author evidently is a follower of Jesus and has a concern for Jewish Christians in the Dispersion. A date for the writing of 1 Peter is probably 95-120 CE.

A **thesis** for 1 Peter is: **Prepare for the soon coming of the Kingdom of God.**

Some of the salient points are these. Being "sprinkled by the blood of Christ" is part of the writer's salutation. He does not elaborate. In some of the Mystery religions of that era, it was the practice to sprinkle the blood of an animal on the initiate. In Jewish religion the blood of sacrificed animals was the symbol of life-giving power, although for a Jew, hence Jewish Christians, to be sprinkled by the blood would have been sacrilegious. There is no evidence that any of the Christian churches used actual blood in their rites, but this book and other New Testament books refer to the blood of Jesus and its salvific power.

According to 1 Peter, being in Christ is one's hope for salvation. Such a person must lead a righteous life, be subject to the government, even "honor the Emperor"—a puzzling admonition since Domitian recently had been anti-Christian.

1 Peter also tells slaves to be subject to their masters. While slavery in those days was not usually a life-indenture as it was in early America, it was a servitude that was not the first choice of slaves.

The document reflects the late first century bias in the church to install men as the leaders of the church. No explanation is given in the New Testament for this bias. A likely cause was the example of the Roman Empire itself, which was an exclusively male combine. 1 Peter exhorts the women to obey their husbands and to remember that women are the weaker sex.

1 Peter encourages Christians to be ready to undergo persecution (apparently a reference to persecution by imperial order), a seeming contradiction to the earlier passage to honor the Emperor.

1 Peter exhorts Christians to accept suffering, for the "end" of this age is "near." The current "fiery ordeal" is puny compared to the triumph about to come with the entry of the Kingdom of God. The "devil" prowls around like a lion to devour the faithful, so be alert.

With greetings that seem to imitate some of the writings of Paul, the book closes.

James

A book of Exhortation with some variation from the previous works is James.

This book may have gotten into the Christian New Testament by mistake. Consider that it is addressed to the "twelve tribes in the Dispersion." Also consider that there are only two scant references to Jesus or Christ in the entire five chapters. Also consider that James' view of good works as the measure of salvation is diametrically opposed to Paul's view—this is a mighty collision of theology.

It is possible that James was intended for the Dispersion proper instead of for Christians. Those two scant references to Jesus and Christ may have been inserted later by churchmen who assumed that since Jesus had a brother named James that this book was written by that brother. Also, the Jewish Christians did think that good works were vital; they may have appropriated this book to influence the Christian movement in that direction. Also consider that the title "Lord" is used thirteen times in James, but the title could be applied to God rather than to Jesus; the title "God" is used fifteen times and all of these apply to God, not Jesus; and the three mentions of "Father" all are in connection with God.

Furthermore, there are many references from the Hebrew Bible (Old Testament): "care for orphans and widows," "law," "God is one," "Abraham," "prophets," "Job," and "Elijah." Other passages of length sound like Hebrew Bible passages.

With the exception of the two scant references to Jesus, James could be a normal book of the Hebrew Bible rather than the Christian New Testament.

If you turn in the Appendix of my book to the entry, "Marks of the Church," and under it the topic, "Canon," you can see that James was on the "doubtful status" list as late as the 300's CE. How it finally was included in the Christian canon is not a matter of historical record.

Since it is included in the New Testament, we will treat it.

The tradition that claims James the brother of Jesus wrote this book cannot be substantiated. Several factors negate this tradition. Among them is that James was martyred before the Jewish-Roman War which began in 66 BCE. Another is that the brothers of Jesus probably were illiterate; even Jesus wrote nothing except one little scribble in the sand. Even if his brother James were literate, he would be literate in Aramaic, not in Greek; Greek is the language of this book. The naming of James in the first verse makes no claim that this James is the brother of Jesus. There were several men called James mentioned in the New Testament. James was a common name in that era. James was a good Jewish name, which makes it appropriate for this book.

Another intriguing postulate among scholars about the book is that it is a cut-and-paste composition. The content is a compendium of materials. They appear to have been gathered and assembled in a collage manner, rather than created by original writing. Thus, James is an edited volume of practical exhortation from a highly Jewish oriented anonymous author.

The book appears to have been written sometime between 95 and 140 CE.

The book lends itself to a simple **thesis**: **Do good works.**

James exhorts his audience to withstand "trials of any kind" by meeting them with good works. A list of the "trials" includes lack of wisdom, doubt, poverty, speaking before thinking, anger, sloth, unbridled tongues, orphans and widows in distress, favoritism, lack of mercy, hypocritical teachers, envy, selfish ambition, lack of peace, worldliness, pride, judging of others, fraud, impatience, oath making, lack of praying and singing, and wandering away from the truth.

The author repeats his command to his readers to do good works; do them now, today, for tomorrow is uncertain.

In 5:14 James mentions the elders of the church who should pray over and anoint the sick; but outside of the word "church" this ministry of the elders would not be new to Jews.

A little tack is put on the end of the book. It offers a kind of extra credit to the doing of good works. Whoever goes after and brings back a sinner from wandering from the truth, not only will save the sinner's soul, but also will "cover a multitude of sins." This statement is not explained. Does it refer to the saver's sins? Does it refer to the sinner's sins? Does it refer to social, national, or cosmic sins? There is no explanation. This passage also suggests an awarding of merit and a bestowing of rewards that seem out of keeping with the other books of the New Testament.

In summary, while the book of James is included in the Christian scriptures, it presents a multitude of problems. On the positive side, it offers many excellent suggestions for righteous living. It exhorts readers to do good works, certainly a worthy endeavor for both the greatest and the least in the Kingdom of God.

1 John

The apparent reason for this Exhortation being written is that there are internal threats to the health of the "little children." These threats are lack of fellowship, sin, love of the world, antichrists, love that does not express itself in action, spirits who do not confess that Jesus has come in the flesh, and more sin. It appears that the churches of the author's acquaintance were not admirable expressions of the Kingdom of God. Thus, not only the uniqueness of the church, but also the very life of the church is being threatened. If the author has read other Christian works, such as Ephesians, he may be thinking that the churches to which he is writing are far from being the body of Christ on Earth. They are far from being the Kingdom come.

The book speaks of the church, its members, and its setting in the world in such a way that it could be dated in the first part of the second century, 100-135 CE. The place from which it was written is unknown, but it sounds as if it could come from Asia Minor, or a bit less likely from Alexandria.

1 John is the first of three letters attributed to "John." Actually, "John" is never mentioned in the letter: someone, sometime attached the name of John to this book. What John from where, who should be so honored with a sacred book, has not been settled. John was a common name in those times, even as it is now.

What can be said are some inferences about the author. Evidently the author is an older Christian who has seen both good times and bad times for the church. Now the author sees bad times. There are external threats and internal threats to the church, but in John's opinion the internal threats get the edge. He writes to no one in particular, but perhaps to everyone in general. Presumably the book is addressed to churches and Christians who will read it. Who these are is never said. The book gives only this address, "little children."

1 John has several exhortations. Three notable ones could be combined in this **thesis**: **Do not sin, love one another, and believe in Christ Jesus.**

Chapter 1 has these noteworthy concepts: "word of life," "God is light," and "blood of Jesus."

Chapter 2 speaks of "my little children" as if the writer is an overseer, perhaps an elder, presbyter, or bishop (or a "metropolitan" bishop, first mentioned in non-canonical literature about 100 CE, who oversaw the house churches in a highly populated area). The author mentions fathers and young people, as if he is the shepherd of all ages in his church or in his city.

The author warns the church about "antichrists," that is, those who oppose its teachings, who do not practice its love of members for each other, who are not committed to the belief that Jesus is the Son of God, and/or who live in "darkness."

Chapters 2 to 4 develop the characterization of antichrists as ones who teach falsely about the very person of Jesus. These falsely assert that the divine Jesus did not become a human being in the flesh. As we have noted previously, there were Gnostic Christians who insisted that since God was spirit, that Jesus, if he were God, also was spirit. Therefore, the real Jesus could not have been incarnated because that would have meant that Jesus would have become less than God. Furthermore, it would have meant that Jesus would have taken on the sinful nature that all other human beings had. If so, then Jesus would be at least partly sinful, no matter how good he was otherwise.

Some Christians carried this line of thinking further. The Docetic Christians declared that Jesus, as far as his flesh part went, was an apparition rather than a reality. Jesus wore the mask of humanity so that humans might see him, and thus see God. Jesus even could have eaten fish or slept on the ground or hugged his mother; but these would be part of the "appearance" of Jesus and not his divine reality. John exhorts his readers to refute all the false teaching about Jesus not really becoming flesh.

In chapter 3 the book insists that those who are in Christ cannot sin. If he really means this, then the church roll would have to be cut severely, for he notes extensive sin within the church. The author further exhorts his readers to love one another and to help one another.

Chapter 4 carries on about spirits. What he means is not clear, but it must have been clear to the readers in his day. The author declares that those whom God loves and who respond to that love by loving one another receive the Holy Spirit—a requirement for receiving the Holy Spirit at least stated differently from the original manner of receiving the Holy Spirit on Pentecost or in the churches founded by Paul.

The author uses an expression that became normative in the church, "confess" that Jesus is the Christ, the Son of God. "Confession" of faith, or "confession" of the faith, became the way of distinguishing between "believers" and non-Christians.

The last chapter of 1 John exhorts readers to believe in the Son in order to have eternal life with the Father. The wording is reminiscent of The Gospel According to John.

The author then mentions "mortal" and "not mortal" sins. This is a new wrinkle in the qualitizing of sins.

The book closes by admonishing the little children to keep themselves from "idols." No explanation of idols is given. There follows only a period.

Jude

Jude is an Exhortation to Christians to be obedient. Its **thesis** is: **Obey the moral teachings of Christ.**

Jude is such a short book that it does not have chapters; only verses, twenty-five of them. It has presented problems to scholars in that it claims to be the composition of one who is the brother of James, the brother of Jesus, which would make Jude a brother of Jesus, too. The Gospels do mention the names of the brothers of Jesus, and one of them is Jude.

The author, however, does not call himself a brother of Jesus. The book quite probably does not come from a brother of Jesus or from anyone in that generation. It does call on those who are "beloved in God" to heed the words of the Apostles; this indicates that the book was written in the following generation, or even later. Passages in Jude about spurious teachings indicate a late date for its composition: 140 CE is not out of the question.

The from where and the to whom are not specifically named in the book. There is only a general salutation to those whom God is keeping "safe for Jesus."

The author exhorts readers to contend for the "faith" that was delivered once and for all to the saints. This is a content meaning for "faith." Faith for Jude is correct beliefs, especially in regard to the moral teachings of Christ. This is a tremendous switch from the early Christian definition of faith as trust. This definition of faith by Jude signals a trend that became dominant by the fourth century: in 325 CE the Council of Nicea made a long list of all the correct beliefs for Christians and called it "The Creed."

Jude warns of false teachers who accept Christ's mercy, but who turn around to do licentious things. Especially condemned are those who lust, use "bombastic speech," and practice flattery. Those who do these things, says Jude, are devoid of the Holy Spirit.

Jude calls upon the Christians to pray to God who is able to keep them from falling and able to present them without blemish to his presence. Such presentable Christians are those who obey the moral teachings of Christ.

2 Peter

The last of the Exhortations and probably the last book of the New Testament to be written is 2 Peter.

The book is a strongly worded document. Its **thesis** is: **Adhere to the Apostolic teaching.**

2 Peter is unique. It appears to be an attempt to acknowledge that Christianity is no longer Jewish, and yet it guards against Christianity being too Gentile.

It acknowledges that the Kingdom of God has not come. The Jewish background of eschatological expectation and the succeeding Christian expectation enunciated by the Apostles has not materialized. Nevertheless, the Apostles were not wrong. The Kingdom is coming—but it may take awhile. Any delay will seem like a long time only because of human measurement. God is delaying the Parousia in God's good time in order that all may have time to repent and enter the Kingdom. When the Kingdom does come it will do so in a cacophonous fire that will dissolve everything and replace Earthly existence with a new Heavens and a new Earth where righteousness "is at home." The book asserts that the Apostolic teaching about this is not in error; only the schedule is pliant.

2 Peter alludes to Hellenistic thinking about the efficacy of virtue as contrasted with trusting faith. The book lists qualities of virtue that might be found in Hellenistic writings, such as goodness, knowledge, self-control, and endurance. This signifies that the writer no longer thought it necessary to tie Christianity to the parent religion of Judaism.

The book makes pungent attacks on unChristlike behavior. It calls sinners, "Accursed children!" It compares those who become Christians and then transgress as pigs who are washed but return to wallowing in the mud. The author exhorts Christians to straighten up and be good. Their "call" and "election" can be nullified by immorality. Then the book turns harsh on this topic. It likens sinners to animals that are "born to be caught and killed!"

2 Peter continues its admonition to adhere to the Apostolic teaching. Not only the teaching on correct morality but also the teaching on correct belief must be followed. Christians must reject the incorrect teachings being circulated in the church, and observe the right teachings if they want to be part of the Kingdom of God. Of a certainty, God will punish those who heed or teach the false.

This pseudonymous book was included in the Christian canon, then excluded from the canon, and finally included in the canon. Apparently those who debated the canon were aware that this book was not written by the Apostle Peter, inasmuch as the book itself makes reference to the writings of Paul, and then speaks of "other scripture" as if Paul's have had time to become regarded as scripture. Only about the year 140 CE were the letters of Paul collected by Marcion as if they were worthy of preservation.

The author overdoes it a bit in chapter 3 by implying that he is one of Jesus' Apostles. He claims that his book is a "second letter" that he has written to whomever he is writing.

A reasonable estimation for the date of the writing of 2 Peter is the year 150; and this is a reasonable date for the last of the literature that was included in the New Testament

The book closes with a blessing on the readers, a final exhortation to shun erroneous teaching, and an expression of praise to the Lord and Savior Christ Jesus "to the day of eternity."

The book also closes our study.

Christianity

Appendices

Chronology of Israel/Palestine

Date (approx.)	Event	Reading
BCE		
356-323	Alexander the Great	1 Macc.
323-197	Ptolemys of Egypt	1 Macc.
197-165	Seleucids of Syria	2 Macc.
165-63	Hasmonians, Chanukkah	1,2 Macc., Dan.
63	Pompey, Romans	
37-4	Herod the Great	
30 BCE-14 CE	Octavian (Caesar Augustus)	
8/5 BCE-27/29 CE	John the Baptist	Mt., Mk., Lk., Jn.
7/4 BCE-29/30 CE	Jesus	Mt., Mk., Lk., Jn.
4 BCE-39 CE	Herod Antipas over Galilee	Mk., Lk.
CE		
0/5-64/65	Saul/Paul	Acts, Gal.
14-37	Tiberius Emperor	Lk.
26-36	Pontius Pilate Prefect Judea	Mt., Mk., Lk., Jn.
41-44	Herod Agrippa I over Judea	Acts
41-54	Claudius Emperor	Acts
49	Jews banished from Rome	Acts
49	Jerusalem Conference	Acts, Gal.
50/52	1 Thes. first NT writing	1 Thes.
54-68	Nero Emperor	
62	James martyred	Acts
66-74	Jewish-Roman War	
81-96	Domitian Emperor	Rev.
90	Hebrew/Jewish Bible closed	
98-117	Trajan Emperor	
110	Pliny correspondence	
117-138	Hadrian Emperor	
132-135	Bar Cochba Revolt	
150	2 Pet. last NT writing	2 Pet.

Churches by 150 CE

(<u>Sources:</u> New Testament; Eusibius, <u>The History of the Church</u>)

A. Cities

- Alexandria
- Amastius
- Antioch of Syria
- Athens
- Caesarea
- Cenchrea
- Colossae
- Corinth
- Edessa (?)
- Ephesus
- Gortyna
- Hierapolis
- Jerusalem/Aelia
- Laodicea
- Lyons (?)
- Magnesia
- Nicomedia
- Nicopolis
- Pella
- Pergamum
- Philadelphia
- Philippi
- Philomelim
- Ptolemais
- Rome
- Sardis
- Smyrna
- Sparta
- Thessalonica
- Thyatira
- Tralles
- Troas
- Tyre
- Vienne (?)

B. Regions

- Achaia
- Asia
- Bithynia
- Cappadocia
- Crete
- Cyprus
- Dalmatia
- Egypt
- Ethiopia
- Galatia
- Galilee
- Gaul
- Illyricum
- Judea
- Palestine
- Parthia
- Perea
- Phrygia
- Pontus
- Samaria
- Scythia

Dates of the New Testament Books

(Dates are approximate)

50-52	1 Thessalonians	1 Thes.
52-54	1 Corinthians	1 Cor.
53-55	2 Corinthians	2 Cor.
55	Galatians	Gal.
56-58	Romans	Rom.
58-62	Philippians	Philip.
58-62	Philemon	Philem.
68-70	Mark	Mk.
85	Matthew	Mt.
90	Luke	Lk.
90	Acts	Acts
90-95	Hebrews	Heb.
90-100	Colossians	Col.
90-120	2 Thessalonians	2 Thes.
90-130	Ephesians	Eph.
95	Revelation	Rev.
95-120	1 Peter	1 Pet.
95-140	James	Jas.
100-120	1 Timothy	1 Tim.
100-120	Titus	Tit.
100-120	2 Timothy	2 Tim.
100-120	John	Jn.
100-135	1 John	1 Jn.
100-150	2 John	2 Jn.
100-150	3 John	3 Jn.
140	Jude	Jude
150	2 Peter	2 Pet.

Festivals of the Church

There were two festivals celebrated by the early church. They were the resurrection day and the birthday of Jesus.

1. Resurrection Day/Easter.

When the church began, the members met daily for a short time, and then met weekly on the first day of the week because that was the day of the week on which Jesus was resurrected.

At an unknown date, probably early in the second century, Jesus Followers began making resurrection day into a festival. By the year 160 CE the church in Rome was celebrating resurrection day in the late winter/early spring. The Council of Nicea in 325 CE, no doubt at the request or order of Emperor Constantine, standardized the date as the first Sunday following the first full moon after the Spring equinox (the day when the sun's path in the sky crosses the equator, thus making days and nights of equal length). This means that the date can range between March 22 and April 25. Some of the churches in the eastern part of the Empire contested the dating set at Nicea and set their own date; yet apparently all churches were observing a festival of the resurrection of Jesus by 325.

At some point the festival came to be called "Easter." This name has a variety of connections. In the eastern part of the Roman Empire and/or in Saxon territory, a spring festival was observed in honor of the goddess of fertility. The goddess was named "Estare"/"Eastre"/"Ostara"/"Oestre" (and probably other local spellings). The goddess was the lord of fertility and the celebration was in thanksgiving for the renewal of the spring growth of crops. The bunny rabbit was said to be a symbol of the goddess; the rabbit could lay colored eggs which were hunted and enjoyed by children. The church united this celebration with the resurrection of Jesus—the pre-Christian celebration was too popular to be eliminated, so it was incorporated.

2. Birthday/Christmas.

The second festival was for the birthday of Jesus. How soon this celebration was begun in the church is not a matter of historical record. It is reasonable to assume that there was no concern with Jesus' birthday in the beginning because Jesus was expected to return momentarily. When Jesus didn't return year after year someone, somewhere, sometime, suggested honoring Jesus with a birthday celebration on his human birth date. Probably celebrations were begun in the early second century when it was assumed more widely that Jesus was not coming again, at least soon.

By this time, however, the exact date was not known. The real date of Jesus birth doubtfully was on or near December 25. If the birth story of Jesus given by The Gospel According to Luke is historical, a census in all probability would not have been ordered at the depth of winter.

It seems to be the case that December 25 was chosen because there was a pre-Christian festival on or about December 25 that celebrated the return of the sun after the shortest day of the year. This winter solstice was a logical time for hope to be reborn when there had been anxiety that the days might keep getting shorter and darker until everything went out. Among the Romans this festival was called the Saturnalia/Sol Invictus. Other peoples had similar celebrations at this time of the year. The church at an unknown date, probably at varying dates in various locales, began combining the pre-Christian celebrations with the birthday of Jesus; this was a logical time for Jesus as the light of the world to be born (reborn).

At any rate, the historical record from Rome attests that December 25 was celebrated by the church there in the year 336. In the Eastern churches the celebration was on January 6, but a beginning date for the celebration in the Eastern churches is not extant. December 25 became more widely kept than January 6, although neither date is universal to our day.

Kingdom of God

The Kingdom of God is a vital concept in biblical Christianity. The concept stems from the Jewish religion preceding the time of Jesus. From Abraham onward there was the expectation that the Hebrews (later called "Jews") would be a Kingdom under God. During the times of the classical Hebrew kings, David and successors, the Hebrews were an autonomous kingdom; it was hoped that such a kingdom would have not only political but also religious integrity, hence be a Kingdom of God.

At times such an ideal Kingdom seemed within reach. Then the Babylonians invaded Israel in the sixth century BCE and interrupted the reach for such a Kingdom. The Babylonians took leading religious Jews into exile. In Babylon the Jews composed literature to keep the concept alive in the minds of the people; many of these writings are preserved in the Jewish Bible (the Christian "Old Testament").

After the Babylonian Exile, the Jews were unable to establish either an independent national kingdom or a righteous Kingdom of God or a unification of the two. The Jews largely were made subservient to more powerful foreign regimes.

In the second century BCE the Jewish Hasmonean family led a revolt against the successors to Alexander the Great. The Hasmoneans reestablished the independent sovereignty of Israel, instituted the festival of Chanukkah, and appeared to be the promised messiahs to bring about the ideal Kingdom—united politically and righteously.

It was not to be. The Hasmonean leadership deteriorated. The dynasty contested viciously within itself for the right to rule politically. In addition it usurped the high priesthood, and that office became more like a political plum than a seat of righteousness. The political independence was ended by the Romans in 63 BCE.

The hope for political independence did not wane, however, and a hundred years later the Jews began an armed rebellion against the Romans. The Jews lost the war. Still the longing for independence did not die. The Jews began another armed rebellion against Rome in 132 CE, and this time the Jews were completely defeated and driven from Palestine. No Jewish political kingdom arose again until the twentieth century with the establishment of the state of Israel.

The sentiment for a unified realm of political independence and divine righteousness was very strong during the time of Jesus. The problem facing such sentiment was two-fold: the Romans, and human sin. The Romans held sway politically. Human sin among the Jews was as prolific as ever both personally and systemically.

Several differing voices were raised among the Jews as to how to overcome these two folds of the problem. Some Jews, such as the Zealots, proclaimed that God would empower them to expel the Romans. Other Jews, such as the Pharisees, proclaimed that complete obedience to God could start at the grass-roots and grow from within to the fullness of righteousness and freedom from sin. Others, such as the peasants, were ready for any change that promised any better state of affairs. One aspect of all such hope was that of God's role. God had intervened in human history before to redeem his chosen people. Surely God could do it again.

Along came Jesus. He worked on the righteous Kingdom of God fold. He proclaimed that God was about to establish a Kingdom that would be righteous; he gave little attention to the political aspect, as if it didn't matter or as if it would be a natural outcome of the righteous dimension. Jesus looked for God's intervention, soon. "Repent, for the Kingdom of God is at hand," was his first exhortation.

Some people were convicted by Jesus' preaching, and others were attracted to his charismatic person and work. While Jesus indicated that there would be one sent by God later to bring the Kingdom, some Jews transferred the identity of that one to Jesus himself.

In spite of Jesus' execution on charges of sedition and blasphemy, his closest followers decided that he was the one, the Messiah, whom God had ordained to establish the Kingdom. Those same followers were divided on how and when the Kingdom of God would be realized. Some thought it would be cataclysmic and would happen in their lifetimes. When Jesus himself did not return to establish a Kingdom in cataclysmic fashion, many of his followers believed that he and/or God would send their Holy Spirit to guide in the establishment of the Kingdom. The coming of the Holy Spirit did occur on the founding day of the church, Pentecost 29/30 CE. (Specifics about Jesus, Holy Spirit, and church varied with the Jesus Followers; see the Appendix in this book, "Varieties of Christianity.")

Others thought that since no cataclysm happened immediately, Jesus must have meant a long-term coming of the Kingdom, a coming that began in individual hearts and spread like a mustard seed growing until righteousness flourished everywhere; then the Kingdom will have come.

As the years passed and still Jesus had not come a second time, a concept began to grow that the Kingdom would never come to Earth, but would be located in Heaven and be populated by the Jesus Followers who died and were "caught up…in the air." In Heaven, with God, Jesus ruled for sure. In Heaven there would be no secular, political competition. In Heaven existence would be free from fleshly, sinful limitations. Heaven would be righteous in the ultimate sense. In fact, it would need no political aspect to guarantee its independence. God /Jesus would rule, and rule righteously. Heaven would be eternal. The Kingdom of God would be there, not here.

Marks of the Church—Office, Creed, Canon

There were three marks that made a church a church in early Christianity. At first there were varieties in all of the three marks. As the years passed the marks were standardized by the dominant variety of Christianity.

1. Office.

One mark of the church was office. On the very first day of the church the Apostles did the leading and took care of crowd control. Soon there arose a need for table servers to see that food was distributed equitably. Seven men were chosen to fill this office. After a few years the church came under the leadership of James, a brother of Jesus. How he was chosen for the office and exactly what the duties of his office were are not stated.

The churches Paul founded had no official governors. The members expected to receive various functional gifts from the Holy Spirit, and then were to express those gifts for the benefit of the entire congregation. The gifts were given both to men and to women (there is no word on the children or how old children had to be to take membership and be gifted). Those who taught and evangelized were given recognition, although they were given no titled official status.

Christians who came from the Jewish tradition probably were the first to choose Elders/aka Presbyters, since Judaism recognized older men of experience and wisdom already as "Elders" who could give counsel and judgment.

By the end of the first century, after Paul and the Apostles were dead, and after Jesus had not returned to lead the church, the local churches began filling offices. The fluid method of Paul in relying on every person to do right and exercise gifts appropriately did not work over the long haul; frequently it resulted in clashes over policies and practices within local churches.

The office of Elder/Presbyter spread among the churches. This office was expected to give spiritual and unifying leadership. In time, the office of Bishop was created; sometimes this office appears to have been equivalent to Elder/Presbyter. It probably grew out of the office of Elder/Presbyter. Later it was considered a higher office than Elder/Presbyter. By the second century the Bishops of major cities were exercising a kind of archbishop or metropolitan bishop function: they advised and decreed for more churches than just their individual congregations.

At the turn of the first century, the New Testament "Pastoral Letters" of 1 Timothy, 2 Timothy, and Titus were written. These give lengthy qualifications for the offices of Elder and Deacon; apparently the office of Deacon was a successor to the Servers inasmuch as Deacons performed the more mundane ministries, as contrasted with the more spiritual ministries of the Elders/Presbyters.

Furthermore, the Pastoral Letters restrict these offices to males, a restriction that was not made in the beginning years of the church. Paul especially is noted for according women the same leadership gifts and status as men. As the years passed, however, the dominant party in Christianity followed a policy of eliminating women from leadership roles.

The first officers probably served without pay. Later they served with pay. The record is not specific about when the switch to paid officers became the norm. The churches no doubt varied in their payment of officers.

In the second century, as the churches were struggling for survival and for orthodoxy of belief, the requirement of apostolic succession became important. Apostolic succession meant that Jesus chose Apostles, then the Apostles chose leaders, then those leaders chose other leaders, and so on. As the years passed it became the norm that to be an authorized leader, a person needed to be in this line of succession. The following is a list of known offices in early Christianity:

1. Jesus, the Messiah/Christ/Anointed One.
2. Twelve Disciples/Apostles.
3. Servers chosen by Jerusalem Church, this office probably evolved into Deacons.
4. Elders/Presbyters.
5. Bishops.

Other gifted leaders were apostles (beyond the Twelve), evangelists, pastors, prophets, and teachers. These probably weren't official offices in the early church.

2. Creed.

Another mark of the church was creed. At the beginning of the church in 29/30 CE Peter invited persons to repent and accept Jesus as the Messiah sent by God. This was part faith action and part belief action. That is, it was a trust type of response as well as an assent to propositions about Jesus type of response.

The faith part was simple to maintain, that is, it need not change with the passing years. All converts had to do was acknowledge that they trusted in Christ.

The belief part became complicated. As more and more members were added to the church—often members who had no background in Jesus' native Jewish religion or in any religion—the need became obvious for basic beliefs to be enunciated.

The earliest creedal statement on record was "Jesus is Lord," also known as the "Old Roman Symbol." The next assertion about Jesus was that he was the "Christ." Christ is the Greek word for "Messiah," both of which mean "anointed one." Kings were anointed to their rule. Prophets could be anointed. A Christ was one specially commissioned to carry out the will of God. The term is a title, so it should precede the name in this way: "Christ Jesus," in the same way that Christians would say, "Lord Jesus."

Soon other additions were made to a profession of belief about Jesus and/or God and/or the church. One of the early additions was about the resurrection. Another was about participants in the passion of Jesus. Others were about his birth and upbringing. Others were on the nature of God and the work of the Holy Spirit. Others described the salvation and destiny of believers.

Several of the New Testament books warn about false teachings. They counsel that certain beliefs are necessary in order for a person to be a correct Christian. Those who do not hold these beliefs are designated false believers, antichrists, and before the turn of the second century, heretics.

There are several short creedal statements in a few New Testament books. None of these evidently covered all belief aspects thought necessary by the dominant variety of Christianity.

An early unofficial creed is called the "Apostles Creed." It developed about a century or so after the Apostles. The time and place of its formulation are unknown, but the Creed has been retained in usage to our day. In one edition, it reads:

"I believe in God almighty And in Christ Jesus his only son our Lord Who was born of the Holy Spirit and the Virgin Mary Who was crucified under Pontius Pilate and buried and the third day rose from the dead Who ascended into heaven and sitteth on the right hand of the Father Whence he cometh to judge the living and the dead And in the Holy Ghost The Holy church The remission of sins The resurrection of the flesh The life everlasting."

Constantine the Great, who was the first Roman Emperor to convert to Christianity, saw the divisiveness that uncertainty or wrangling over beliefs could produce. He wanted unity in his empire. He convened the Council of Nicea in 325 CE and let it be known that he wanted a universal creed. The Council was composed of leading bishops of the church who were of a mind to please the Emperor and compose a catholic creed. They formulated what has become known as the "Nicene Creed." It is the norm for the type of Christianity that has become dominant. It is lengthier than the Apostles Creed, but the two are in general agreement. Both have been used widely by Christians from the time of their composition to our own day. In one edition, the Nicene Creed states:

"We believe in one God the Father almighty maker of heaven and earth and of all things visible and invisible And in one Lord Jesus Christ the only-begotten Son of God begotten from the Father before all ages light from light true God from true God begotten not made of the same substance as the Father through whom all things were made Who for us and for our salvation came down from heaven and was incarnate from the Holy Spirit and the Virgin Mary and was made man and was crucified for us under Pontius Pilate and suffered and was buried and rose the third day according to the scriptures and ascended into heaven and sits on the right hand of the Father and is coming again with glory to judge both living and dead whose Kingdom shall have no end And in the Holy Spirit the Lord and giver of life who proceeds from the Father who with the Father and the Son is jointly worshipped and jointly glorified who spoke through the prophet And in one holy catholic and apostolic church We acknowledge one baptism for the forgiveness of sins We look for the resurrection of the dead and the life of the world to come Amen."

3. Canon.

A third mark of the church was canon. The term is derived from the Greek word "kanon" which comes from "kane" which means "straight reed." The term was used to denote a measure or a rule that designated when something was straight, correct, or measured up to a standard.

In Christian use it came to signify an authoritative catalog of documents that were correct measures of the Christian faith. The term is used in Galatians 6:16 as "rule." There is not a record of the term "canon" being used to denote holy scripture until the fourth century when such leaders as Athanasius in 367 or Amphilochius in 395 used it.

When the church in the beginning referred to scriptures, it meant the Jewish Bible. The first Christians cited the Jewish Bible as their authoritative religious literature.

The earliest non-Jewish, Christian literature on record is that of the correspondence of Paul and his mission team beginning about 50 CE. These letters were instructions to local churches on matters of faith and order. The first record of this literature being collected and viewed as being especially authoritative was about the year 140 when Marcion of Rome made a collection of Pauline correspondence, and portions of The Gospel According to Luke and The Acts of the Apostles.

By the end of the second century there were many Christian writings. Apparently some church leaders thought it was important to distinguish the better ones from the worse ones, and so made preferred lists. Bishop Irenaeus of Lyon is said to have commented about the year 190 that the criteria for having four Gospels about Jesus were that there were four winds in the world and four corners of the Earth.

Scholars have tried to find more substantive criteria for such lists, but at our distance of many centuries the criteria are speculative. The most reasonable ones appear to be these: 1)were the writings consonant with known information about Jesus and/or the early church? 2)were the writings older rather than newer? 3)were the writings connected to the Apostles or to persons associated or thought to be associated with them? 4)were they in general use in churches? 5)could they be normative for the church and Christians? An unknown factor is the degree of church political influence involved, such as primacy assertions of bishops or power struggles between congregations.

In 367 Bishop Athanasius of Alexandria issued his 39th Festal Letter in which he listed the twenty-seven books of the current New Testament. About 396/7 this list was ratified at a provincial church council held in Carthage. The council was not ecumenical, however, so some churches, especially in Syria, contested the inclusion of some of the books for centuries. Even in our day there is disagreement: some churches aver that additional books should be included in the canon.

This New Testament was added to the Bible of the Jews. Christians renamed the Bible as the "Old Testament." The Old Testament was kept by the dominant stream of Christianity as scripture not only because of Jewish heritage, but also because it lent itself to reinterpretation by Christians as heralding the advent and work of a messiah, in this case, Jesus. Those who accepted the Old Testament gave it a status just below that of the New Testament. Some Christians, such as the Marcionites, never accepted the Old Testament at all.

The term "New Testament" probably was used first by Irenaeus, Bishop in Gaul, about 180. He designated the Jewish Bible as the "Old Testament." Tertullian about the year 200 used the term "New Testament" extensively. The concept of a New Testament probably came from the Bible book of Jeremiah chapter 31, which speaks of a New Covenant to be established by God. Christians thought of themselves as a new people in a New Covenant; the word "covenant" could be translated as "testament."

Following is a chronological evolution of the canon into the generally accepted twenty-seven books of the New Testament (most dates are approximate):

140 CE. Various works about Jesus, Christianity, and Church were being collected by individuals and churches.

200 CE. Works being used in the church at Rome, according to the Muratorian Canon:

Matthew
Mark
Luke
John
Acts
Romans
1 Corinthians
2 Corinthians
Galatians
Ephesians
Philippians
Colossians
1 Thessalonians
2 Thessalonians
1 Timothy
2 Timothy
Titus
Philemon

Other works being used in various churches:

James
1 John
2 John
Jude
Revelation
Revelation of Peter
The Shepherd of Hermas
Wisdom of Solomon

250 CE. Works being used by Origen at Alexandria:

- Matthew
- Mark
- Luke
- John
- Acts
- Romans
- 1 Corinthians
- 2 Corinthians
- Galatians
- Ephesians
- Philippians
- Colossians
- 1 Thessalonians
- 2 Thessalonians
- 1 Timothy
- 2 Timothy
- Titus
- Philemon

Other works of questionable status:

- 1 Peter
- 1 John
- Revelation

Other works of doubtful status:

- Hebrews
- James
- 2 Peter
- 2 John
- 3 John
- Jude
- Gospel of the Hebrews
- Letter of Barnabas
- Teaching of the Twelve Apostles
- The Shepherd of Hermas

300 CE. Works being used by Eusibius in Asia Minor:

- Matthew
- Mark
- Luke
- John
- Acts
- Romans
- 1 Corinthians
- 2 Corinthians
- Galatians
- Ephesians
- Philippians
- Colossians
- 1 Thessalonians
- 2 Thessalonians
- 1 Timothy
- 2 Timothy
- Titus
- Philemon

Other works of questionable status:

- 1 Peter
- 1 John
- Revelation

Other works of doubtful status:

- James
- 2 Peter
- 2 John
- 3 John
- Jude

Other works to be excluded:

- Acts of Peter
- Didache
- Gospel of the Hebrews
- Letter of Barnabas
- Revelation of Peter
- The Shepherd of Hermas

367 CE. Works recommended by Bishop Athanasius of Alexandria:

The 27 books in today's generally recognized New Testament.

396/7 CE. The same 27 books as recommended by Athanasius were approved by the Council of Carthage.

Summary

These three marks—office, creed, and canon—were the marks that made a church a church as Christianity developed into the fourth century. If a church, or members of a church, clung to these three marks, then the church was recognized as a true church. If a church or members denied these marks, then the church or members were branded as heretical. In time the "true" churches spoke of their position as being "orthodox," that is, right or correct (practically speaking, it means "winners"). In time the orthodox spoke of their position as being "catholic," that is, world-wide, or total, or universal (practically speaking, it means "winners over all"). By the end of the fourth century the orthodox and catholic variety of Christianity which held to these marks became dominant.

Miracles in Mark, Matthew, Luke

1. Unclean spirit 1:23, -- , 4.33
2. Peter's mother-in-law 1:30, 8:14, 4:38
3. Sick at evening 1:32, 8:16, 4:40
4. Leper 1:40, 8:2, 5:12
5. Paralytic 2:3, 9:2, 5:18
6. Withered hand 3:1, 12:9, 6:6
7. Storm 4:39, 8:23, 8:22
8. Demons to swine 5:1, 8:28, 8:26
9. Ruler's daughter 5:22/35, 9:18/23, 8:40/49
10. Woman with blood 5:25, -- , 8:43
11. Feeding Five Thousand 6:39, 14:13, 9:12
12. Walking on water 6:48, 14:25, --
13. Gentile's daughter 7:24, 15:21, --
14. Deaf mute 7:31, -- , --
15, Feeding Four Thousand 8:1, 15:32, --
16. Blind man 8:22, -- , --
17. Epileptic 9:17, 17:14, 9:38
18. Bartimaeus 10:46, -- , 18:35
19. Two blind men 10:46, 20:30, 18:35
20. Fig tree 11:12, 21:18, --
21. Centurion's servant -- , 8:5, 7:1
22. Two blind men -- , 9:27, --
23. Demon/mute -- , 9:32, --
24. Demon/blind mute -- , 12:22, 11:14
25. Temple tax -- , 17:24, --
26. Escape -- , -- , 4:30
27. Fish -- , -- , 5:1
28. Widow's son -- , -- , 7:11
29. Infirm/bent woman -- , -- , 13:11
30. Dropsy -- , -- , 14:1
31. Ten lepers -- , -- , 17:11
32. Servant's ear -- , -- , 22:51

Parables in Mark, Matthew, Luke

1. New cloth 2:21, 9:16, 5:36
2. New wine 2:22, 9:17, 5:37
3. Sower 4:3, 13:3, 8:5
4. Lamp 4:21, 5:15, 8:16/11:33
5. Growing seed 4:26, -- , --
6. Mustard seed 4:30, 13:31, 13:18
7. Wicked tenants 12:1, 21:33, 20:9
8. Fig tree 13:28, 24:32, 21:29
9. Absentee owner 13:33, -- , --
10. Rock and sand -- , 7:24, 6:47
11. Tares -- , 13:24, --
12. Leaven -- , 13:33, --
13. Hidden treasure -- , 13:44, --
14. Pearl -- , 13:45, --
15. Dragnet -- , 13:47, --
16. Lost sheep -- , 18:12, 15:3
17. Unforgiving servant -- , 18:23, --
18. Laborers -- , 20:1, --
19. Two sons -- , 21:28, --
20. Wedding feast -- , 22:2, --
21. Faithful and evil servants -- , 24:45, 12:42
22. Virgins -- , 25:1, --
23. Talents -- , 25:14, 19:12
24. Creditor and debtors -- , -- , 7:41
25. Good Samaritan -- , -- , 10:30
26. Friend in need -- , -- , 11:5
27. Rich fool -- , -- , 12:16
28. Watchful servants -- , -- , 12:35
29. Fig tree -- , -- , 13:6
30. Great supper -- , -- , 14:16
31. Tower and war -- , -- , 14:28
32. Lost coin -- , -- , 15:8
33. Prodigal son -- , -- , 15:11
34. Unjust steward -- , -- , 16:1
35. Rich man and Lazarus -- , -- , 16:19
36. Unprofitable servants -- , -- , 17:7
37. Persistent widow -- , -- , 18:1
38. Pharisee and tax collector -- , -- , 18:9

Persons of Note

Alexander the Great – Macedonian/Greek 356-323 BCE, conqueror of lands from Europe to India, originator of Hellenism

Annas – Jew, high priest 6-15 CE

Ananias II – Jew, high priest before whom Paul was brought

Antiochus Epiphanes IV – Syrian ruler, attempted to force Hellenism on Israel resulting in Jewish-Syrian War begun 167 BCE, won a few years later by Jews

Apollos – Jew from Alexandria, converted to Christianity c. 50 CE, noted teacher

Aquila – Jew from Rome, converted to Christianity c. 50, with wife Priscilla/Prisca colleague and financial supporter of Paul

Aristotle – Greek 384-322 BCE from Stagira, philosopher, tutor of Alexander the Great, master of many academic disciplines; some of his concepts were used to support Christian doctrine

Augustus – see Gaius Julius Caesar Octavian

Barnabas – Jew, Levite from Cyprus, converted to Christianity c. 50 CE, missionary companion and financial supporter of Paul

Caiaphas – Jew, high priest 18-37 CE

David – Hebrew c. 1040-960 BCE, ideal king of Israel, messianic figure from whose line other messiahs were to come

Democritus – Greek c. 460-370, philosopher, co-founder with Leucippus of classical atomism

Diogenes – Greek c. 400-325 BCE from Sinope, philosopher, rhetorician, itinerate preacher of self-mastery and ethical behavior, popularized diatribe aka "sermon"

Domitian – Roman Emperor 81-96 CE, expected honor to his "divine spirit" which Christians refused to give, probably prosecuted Christians as seditionists

Epicurus – Greek 342-170 BCE, philosopher, counseled mental composure and virtue, advocated atomic cosmology

Felix – Roman, appointed governor of Judea c. 52-60 CE, tried Paul

Festus – Roman, appointed governor of Judea 60-62 CE, present for one of Paul's trials

Gaius Julius Caesar – Roman general, became sole ruler of Rome 49-44 BCE, assassinated on Ides of March by those who opposed monarchical rule

Gaius Julius Caesar Octavian – Roman ruler 31/27 BCE-14 CE

Hasmonians/Maccabees – Jews, led successful revolt against Syria 165 BCE, began dynasty of rulers over Israel

Heraclitus – Greek c. 550-480 BCE, philosopher on change and permanence, began use of term "logos"

Herod the Great – Idumean/Jew, king of Israel 37-4 BCE, firm and sometimes ruthless ruler, great builder, began massive remodeling of Temple

Herod Agrippa I – grandson of Herod the Great, king of various territories north of Israel 37-44 CE, also of Judea and Samaria 41-44 CE

Herod Agrippa II – son of Herod Agrippa I, king of various territories north and east of Israel 50-c. 70 CE

Herod Antipas/Antipater – son of Herod the Great, tetrarch of Galilee and Perea 4 BCE-39 CE

Herod Archelaus – son of Herod the Great, ethnarch of Judea, Samaria, and Idumea 4 BCE-6 CE, banished by Rome for incompetence

Herod Philip – son of Herod the Great, tetrarch of various territories north and east of Israel 4 BCE-34 CE

Isis – Egyptian Goddess of Mystery religion, mother figure

James – 1)one of Jesus' Twelve Disciples 2)James bar Alphaeus one of Jesus' Twelve Disciples 3)brother of Jesus, early leader of church in Jerusalem 4)reputed author of New Testament book

Jeremiah – Jew c. 640-585 BCE, prophet, proposed a New Covenant of heart-felt religion

Jesus – Jew c. 7-4 BCE-29/30 CE

John – 1)Jew, aka John the Baptist, c. 8-5 BCE-27-29 CE, relative and forerunner of Jesus 2)Jew, one of Jesus' Twelve

Disciples 3)reputed author of several New Testament books

Joseph – Jew c. 35 BCE-10 CE, husband of Mary mother of Jesus, carpenter

Joseph of Arimathea – Jew from town ten miles north of Jerusalem, buried Jesus in his family tomb

Josephus, Flavius – Jew c. 37-100 CE, general in Jewish-Roman War, defected to Rome, historian of Jewish events c. 200 BCE-100 CE

Leucippus – Greek c. 500-420 BCE, philosopher, co-founder with Democritus of classical atomism

Maccabees – see Hasmoneans

Marcion – Greek/Roman 85-160 CE, shipping magnate, made first known collection of Paul's writings c. 140 CE, theological dualist

Mary, mother of Jesus – Jew c. 20 BCE-40 CE

Mary, from Magdala – Jew c. 5 BCE-55 CE, companion and financial supporter of Jesus

Moses – Hebrew c. 1300-1200 BCE, leader of Israelites from bondage in Egypt to edge of Israel, Law giver

Nero – Roman Emperor 54-68 CE, prosecuted Christians for great fire in Rome, may have executed Peter and Paul

Nicodemus – Jew, Pharisee, became follower and host of Jesus

Parmenides – Greek c. 515-450 BCE, philosopher on change and permanence

Paul/Saul – Jew c. 0-64/65 CE, converted to Christianity c. 32-35 CE, evangelist, missionary, theologian, advisor, may have been decapitated by Nero; Paul=Latin/Roman name, Saul=Hebrew name

Peter, Simon – Jew c. 0-64/65 CE, one of Jesus' Twelve Disciples, delivered first sermon of the church, may have been crucified by Nero

Philemon – from Asia Minor c. 10-? CE, converted to Christianity by Paul, friend and host to Paul, owner of slave Onesimus

Philo – Jew of Diaspora in Egypt c. 20 BCE-50 CE, philosopher, theologian, synthesized Greek philosophy and Jewish religion

Pilate, Pontius – Roman appointee prefect of Judea 26-36 CE, convicted Jesus of sedition and ordered crucifixion

Plato/Aristocles – Greek 429-347 BCE, philosopher, objective realist (idealist), underlying principle/s of all, theory of Forms, author of Dialogues featuring Socrates

Pliny, the Younger – Roman 61-113 CE, governor of Bithynia, written record c. 110 of request to Emperor Trajan for way to deal with Christianity especially because Christians refused to pray to divine spirit of Emperor

Priscilla/Prisca – Jew from Rome, converted to Christianity c. 50, with husband Aquila colleague and financial supporter of Paul

Pythagoras – Greek c. 570-490 BCE, philosopher, mathematician, metaphysicist

Silas/Sylvanus – probably Gentile who converted to Christianity c. 45 CE, missionary companion of Barnabas, companion and scribe of Paul

Socrates – Greek 470-399 BCE, philosopher of virtue, used dialogue method of defining concepts, executed by poison hemlock for standing for truth

Thales – Greek c. 650-570 BCE, philosopher, cosmologist, abstractionist, coined term "stuff" as essence of universe

Tiberius – Roman Emperor 14-37 CE

Timothy – Jewish mother, Gentile father, converted to Christianity c. 50 CE, assistant and scribe to Paul

Titus – Gentile converted to Christianity c. 52 CE, assistant to Paul

Titus of Rome – Roman Emperor 79-81 CE, general who led Romans to final victory over Jews in 70

Trajan – Roman, Emperor 98-117 CE, corresponded with Pliny, the Younger, about treatment of Christians

Twelve Disciples/Apostles – Jews, chosen by Jesus as assistants; twelve symbolized new Israel; Matthias elected to fill Judas Iscariot's place

Vespasian – Roman Emperor 69-79 CE, general early in Jewish-Roman War

Zeno – Greek from Elea c. 490-420 CE, philosopher, paradoxes on motion, time

Population Statistics

From the birth of Jesus to the time of the writing of the last book of the New Testament about the year 150 CE, the movement known as Christianity or the church developed. From our perspective in the twenty-first century it might seem that the church from the beginning was a vast movement with huge numbers of members. We might forget that the church began from scratch.

The numbers of Christians in the first century have to be estimated by modern scholars because there are no yearbooks of membership from the early years. Consequently the estimates vary considerably. The most reasonable figures seem to be these—be sure to note that all of these are estimates, hopefully educated estimates:

29/30 CE first day of the church, 3,000 claimed; this large figure cannot be substantiated; it is not known if these were one-day repenters or ongoing church members

65 CE about the time of the death of Peter and Paul, probably not more than 10,000; a half-dozen major cities probably had several hundred or more, other cities probably had 100 or fewer

100 CE about the time of the writing of The Gospel According to John, perhaps 20,000

150 CE the time of the end of our study of Christianity in this book, about 50,000

200 CE about the time of the writings of the Christian Apologists, about 100,000

300 CE before the conversion of the Emperor Constantine to Christianity, about 250,000 to 300,000 out of the approximately 50 to 60 million inhabitants of the Roman Empire

325 CE after the conversion of Constantine and the time of the Council of Nicea the numbers skyrocketed; many joined the church because the Emperor did; one story is that Constantine

marched an army through a river and declared them baptized members of the church

396/397 CE the time of the Council of Carthage, about 30 million/50% of the population of the Roman Empire; no doubt many of these were nominal members

Also, it is easy for us to assume that the church had fine buildings in which to meet. It didn't at the beginning. The church met in the homes of its members or in places other than in its own buildings. The earliest building discovered thus far dates from about the year 250 CE, located at Dura-Europos, northeast of Israel. With the conversion of Constantine the construction of church buildings boomed. The rise in construction was caused by several factors, such as 1)Constantine ordered some to be built with public funds; 2)local churches could build without fear of government confiscation of their property; and 3)the huge increase in church membership necessitated larger gathering places than homes.

Also, it is easy to assume that the church was a uniform entity. It was and it wasn't. It was in respect to a basic faith as <u>trust</u> in Jesus as the Christ. It wasn't in respect to faith as <u>belief</u> about Jesus as the Christ. Beliefs varied greatly. Nearly every book in the New Testament presents distinctive nuances of beliefs. The four Gospels are belief-statements, and the four have distinctive theses. It is problematic to try to categorize the beliefs inasmuch as they often overlap. Beliefs run the gamut of a bare separation from Jewish religion to identification with esoteric Greek religions. When Constantine became emperor and converted to Christianity in the fourth century, he wanted a monolithic Christianity to match the monolithic empire. The dominant variety of Christianity responded with rulings on office, creed, and canon. With the power of the throne behind it, the dominant variety enforced its rulings, although minority beliefs trickle throughout church history to the present day.

Rituals of the Church

There were two rituals observed in the church during our period of study. They were baptism and the Lord's Supper.

1. Baptism.

Before Jesus, the Jews performed a type of baptism in the washing ceremony of persons before they performed worship services; the ritual was called "tevilah." Also, the high priest performed immersion of himself in a ritual bath, "mikveh," as a cleansing before conducting the services for Yom Kippur.

The Greek Mystery religions had types of baptism in their initiatory rites. Usually the baptism was by sprinkling or drenching a person with blood or wine.

John the Baptist practiced baptism just prior to the founding of Christianity. John the "Immerser" (literal translation of the Greek word, "Baptist") submersed persons in the Jordan River as the symbol of their willingness to repent and live righteously in the emerging Kingdom of God. Jesus was baptized by John.

Jesus probably adopted John's style of baptism, although the historical records are scanty.

At the founding of the church at the Pentecost Festival in 29/30 CE Peter ordered baptism to be performed on those who accepted Jesus as the Messiah. Peter states very briefly that baptism was for those who repented. If they were baptized in the name of Jesus their sins would be forgiven and they would receive the gift of the Holy Spirit.

The Gospel According to Matthew in the very last verses, called the "Great Commission," implies that baptism was a standard ritual in the church before the end of the first century. Matthew states: "Go therefore and make disciples...baptizing them...." Matthew gives no meaning for baptism. He states that it is to be done in the names of the Father, Son, and Holy Spirit. One implied meaning is that baptism was the entry ritual into the Jesus Way.

Paul and/or his associates evidently administered baptism. The meaning of baptism for Paul may have included the commitments to righteousness stated or implied by all of those mentioned above, but Paul adds the meaning of a mystical union with Christ. Persons who were immersed were symbolically buried and raised in the manner of Christ's death and resurrection, and thus were "united" with Christ.

From Jesus' own baptism on through Paul, baptism was connected with the coming of the Holy Spirit. In the early years of Christianity this meant that the Spirit could and would come immediately on the one baptized and empower the person to perform functionary actions in the church. Paul says more about this than the others. He implies that the empowerments were varied and apparently a person did not know what gift the Holy Spirit was going to bestow until the moment it happened. Some of the usual gifts were teaching, healing, and speaking in such a way that hearers could understand, even if the hearers used some other language.

As the years passed the promise of the immediate gift of the Holy Spirit at the time of baptism dimmed; exactly why is not stated, but perhaps it was because more and more of the people who were baptized were not so righteous as those on the day of Pentecost. They were more like the "sinners still" in the Corinthian church who needed more Christian training before claiming that the Holy Spirit was investing them.

At the beginning of the church, baptism was performed on believers. There is no word on children; since Christianity came out of Judaism it probably considered males to be adults at age twelve.

Baptism in the church was administered by another—it was not self-baptism. It consisted of being immersed in water. Running water was the first choice mentioned in extra-New Testament literature or any pool the next choice. Baptism was observed by Christianity from its birthday onward. It was an essential ritual.

2. Lord's Supper.

The second ritual instituted by the early church was the Lord's Supper. This stemmed from the final meal that

Jesus had with his Twelve Disciples the night before his death. On that occasion the meal was the Seder of the Passover.

Acts 2 says that those who composed the first church met for the "breaking of bread." Other writings in the New Testament speak of the breaking of bread. These passages, however, do not make it clear as to whether a fellowship dinner or a Lord's Supper replica was meant.

By the time of the writing of 1 Corinthians in the 50's CE the ritual side of the breaking of bread had developed into a regular practice, probably observed at every meeting of the members. The members partook of the bread and drank from the cup of juice made from grapes in remembrance of Jesus and as a reminder of the coming Kingdom. The Lord's Supper apparently was the symbolization of ongoing faith in Jesus. It came to be called also "Last Supper," "Table of Thanksgiving," "Communion," and "Eucharist."

1 Corinthians 11 indicates that the Lord's Supper also had acquired sacramental quality for Paul. Rather than just a representation or remembrance of Jesus, the bread "is my body," and the cup "is my blood," implied sacramental meaning. Somehow the bread and the cup conveyed a mystical presence of and union with Jesus.

Summary

The two rituals of the early church were baptism and the Lord's Supper. Baptism was a one time event for a Christian. It was the initial sign of belief in Jesus and commitment to the Christian Way. The Lord's Supper was received by members whenever the church gathered. The Lord's Supper was the continuing sign of being incorporated in the Body of Christ. (Note that Lord's Supper commonly is written with beginning capital letters, but baptism isn't—no known official explanation for this.)

Rulers from Alexander to Constantine

Some of the Major Rulers, World Powers

Alexander, Macedonia/Greece 336-323
Ptolemy Soter I, Egypt 323-283/2
Seleucus Nicator I, Syria 312-281
Antiochus Epiphanes IV, Syria 175-163
Caesar XV and Cleopatra VII, Egypt 44-30
Julius Caesar, Rome 49-44
Octavian, Rome 31/27 BCE-14 CE
Tiberias, Rome 14-37
Nero, Rome 54-68
Vespasian, Rome 69-79
Domitian, Rome 81-96
Trajan, Rome 98-117
Hadrian, Rome 117-138
Marcus Aurelius, Rome 161-180
Decius, Rome 249-251
Diocletian, Rome 284-305
Constantine, Rome 323-337

Some of the minor Rulers, Israel

Herod the Great, king, Israel 40/37-4
Herod Antipas (son of Herod the Great), tetrarch, Galilee and Perea 4 BCE-39 CE
Herod Archelaus (son of Herod the Great), ethnarch, Judea, Samaria, Idumea 4 BCE-6 CE
Herod Philip (son of Herod the Great), tetrarch, territories north and east of Israel 4 BCE-34 CE
Pontus Pilate, prefect, Judea 26-36
Herod Agrippa I (grandson of Herod the Great), king, parts of Israel 37-44
Antonius Felix, governor, Judea 52-60
Porcius Festus, governor, Judea 60-62
Gessius Florus, governor, Judea 64-66

Salvation

Salvation is the term for being freed from evil and freed to righteousness.

In the New Testament salvation has several connotations. In some places it refers to being "cleansed by the blood" of Jesus. Through the self-giving of an innocent human but divine Jesus, the sins of persons are removed by that perfect sacrifice of Jesus.

In other places salvation refers to a state of being in right relationship with God. This state is entered, according to Galatians and Romans, by faith; that is, by trusting in God, trusting in God's good will toward humans, trusting God's power to redeem persons from all iniquities, errors, misfortunes, and even death.

In other places salvation refers to that state of "everyone who believes in him [Christ] may not perish but may have eternal life," as The Gospel According to John puts it.

In other places salvation refers to being a member of the body of Christ, "citizens with the saints and also members of the household of God," as the book of Ephesians says it. Probably most Christians equated "household of God" with the church.

In other places salvation refers to the performance of good works toward other people, as in the books of Matthew and James.

In other places salvation refers to a mystical union with Christ. This is conveyed in such a passage as the one in Romans, "baptized into his death...united with him in a death like his...united with him in a resurrection like his."

In other places salvation refers to having a correct "knowledge" of God.

In other places salvation refers to being in the Kingdom of God.

Salvation has many references in the New Testament era, 30-150 CE. In abstraction, it means being freed from evil and freed to righteousness.

Signs in John

1. Water to wine 2:1
2. Nobleman's son 4:46
3. Infirm man 5:1
4. Feeding the five thousand 6:1
5. Walking on water 6:19
6. Man born blind 9:1
7. Lazarus 11:43
8. Fish 21:4

Theses of the New Testament Books

(In order of probable date of composition)

Mark: Jesus is the serving messiah.
Matthew: Jesus is the teaching messiah.
Luke: Jesus is the compassionate messiah.
John: Jesus is the eternal messiah.
Acts: God is establishing the Kingdom among the obedient.
1 Thessalonians: All faithful Christians shall be saved into the Kingdom of God.
1 Corinthians: Moral Christians shall enter Jesus' soon-coming Kingdom of God.
2 Corinthians: Paul is an authentic apostle of Christ.
Galatians: Grace plus faith equals justification.
Romans: Paul's Christian beliefs and conduct are so correct that the church at Rome ought to contribute financial support for his mission to Spain.
Philippians: Mutual caring prefigures the Kingdom of God.
Philemon: Slave and master are brothers in Christ.
2 John: Love for one another is the true teaching.
3 John: Faithfulness to the truth is good.
1 Timothy: The true church is ordered properly.
Titus: The true church is ordered properly.
2 Timothy: A good church leader opposes false teaching and unchristian behavior.
Hebrews: Follow Jesus the superior messiah.
Colossians: Follow not false teaching.
2 Thessalonians: Be faithful in spite of ill fortune.
Ephesians: Be one Body of Christ.
Revelation: Be faithful in spite of tribulations.
1 Peter: Prepare for the soon coming of the Kingdom of God.
James: Do good works.
1 John: Do not sin, love one another, and believe in Christ Jesus.
Jude: Obey the moral teachings of Christ.
2 Peter: Adhere to the Apostolic teaching.

Traditional Greek/Roman Gods

(The Greek gods came first, then were adopted and renamed by the Romans)

1. Zeus=Jupiter
   (Father, sky, rain, thunderbolt)
2. Hera=Juno
   (Wife, marriage, women)
3. Poseidon=Neptune
   (Sea, water, earthquake, tamer of horses, trident)
4. Apollo=Apollo
   (Manly beauty, music, archery, prophecy, medicine, flocks, herds, law, civilizations, sun, lyre and bow)
5. Artemis=Diana
   (Chastity, childbirth, wild animals)
6. Athena=Minerva
   (Virginity, wisdom, arts)
7. Hermes=Mercury
   (Messenger of the gods, roadways, herdsmen, cleverness, conductor of souls to Hades)
8. Ares=Mars
   (War)
9. Aphrodite=Venus
   (Love, beauty, fertility)
10. Demeter=Ceres
    (Grain)
11. Dionysus=Bacchus
    (Wine)
12. Hephaestus=Vulcan
    (Fire, crafts)

Varieties of Christianity

Christianity as an organized religion is counted by most scholars to have been started at the Festival of Pentecost held in Jerusalem in the year 29/30 CE. The account given in the New Testament book of The Acts of the Apostles describes a dynamic event in which three thousand persons "joined" a movement because they accepted Jesus as the Messiah.

The movement was not confined to Jerusalem, however, since there were many Jewish Diaspora pilgrims in town for the celebration. It is reasonable to assume that the joiners from the Diaspora went back to their homelands and established the movement in those places. At least some of the Apostles (the records of their activities are incomplete) evangelized. Soon the mission teams of Paul and Barnabas extended the movement.

A striking thing about the movement during our scope of study, 29/30-150 CE, is that it was not monolithic, either in faith or in order. There was no central office. Consequently, varying patterns of faith and order developed. The following are some of the major varieties of Christianity to the middle of the second century—the time of the writing of the last book of the New Testament.

1. Jewish Christianity.

Jewish Christianity was the original variety of Christianity. Quite probably all the members of the church founded at the Pentecost Festival in Jerusalem in 29/30 were Jews, either residents of Jerusalem or pilgrims from sites of the Diaspora. They were called simply "Jesus Followers," or "Disciples of Jesus," or "Nazarenes," or "The Way."

The number of Jesus Followers in Jerusalem grew. Leaders were the Apostles Peter, John, James, and a brother of Jesus also named James.

Jewish Christians believed that Jesus would return soon to complete the establishment of the Kingdom of God on Earth. There was no need to keep records since the Messiah would be there to lead. About the year 49 James, the brother of Jesus, presided over a Conference in Jerusalem which made rulings in regard to the inclusion of Gentiles in the Way.

Jewish Christianity revered the Mosaic Law and the Bible (Old Testament) and saw no incongruity in following Jesus as part of their Jewish heritage. They probably intended to start only a new "Party" or sect of Judaism, not a new religion. According to the book of Acts they practiced the teaching, fellowship, breaking of bread, and prayers associated with Jesus while he had been on Earth. They practiced, at first at least, the sharing of their wealth in a common treasury, open to draws according to members' needs. At first they assembled daily.

The Jewish Christians flourished until the Jewish-Roman War in 66-70. A fourth century church historian, Eusibius, claims that the Jewish Christians who did not perish in the War made their way to Pella, a Hellenistic city east of the Jordan River. Eusibius asserts, however, that some Christians returned to Jerusalem later; he gives the names of thirteen successors to James who led the church there in the years 62-135. In 135 Jerusalem again was destroyed in a war with the Romans. This was a further blow to the Jewish Christians and they virtually disappeared from Christian history.

Probably the "Judaizers" mentioned in Paul's letters in the New Testament were Jewish Christians. There were some of these at nearly all the sites where Paul evangelized. The Judaizers opposed Paul on the issue of keeping the precepts of the Jewish Law prior to being full-fledged Disciples of Jesus. Some scholars in our time attribute the New Testament book of James to the Jewish Christians, although this attribution has not been established with certainty.

2. Hellenistic Christianity.

At the founding of the church on the day of Pentecost, there were pilgrims from the Diaspora—sites among the Gentiles where Hellenistic culture was prevalent. Probably most of these persons were Jewish, but they were not as strictly Jewish as the persons who lived in Israel. Some of them may have been Gentiles who had converted to the Jewish religion.

There were some Hellenistic Jesus Followers who either lived in Jerusalem or tarried in Jerusalem to await the coming again of Jesus. The New Testament book of Acts relates the complaint of Hellenistic Followers over the distribution of food and possibly funds. The church there, or at least one of the local units of the church there, appointed seven officers to minister to these members.

Hellenistic Jesus Followers who lived in Antioch, Syria, initiated the missionary journeys of Barnabas, Paul, Silas, Mark, and others. The first time on record that the Followers were called "Christians" was at Antioch. Within a few years, Hellenistic Christianity had spread all the way to Rome.

The Hellenistic Christians did not insist on strict obedience to the Jewish Law. They clashed with the Jewish Christians over this matter, and they probably played a role at the Jerusalem Conference which determined just how much Jewish religion was necessary for persons to have in order to become Christians.

Hellenistic Christianity continued its existence, but was close enough to Gentile Christianity that in time it lost its distinction.

3. Gentile Christianity.

Beginning in the late 40's many Gentiles were brought into the Jesus movement. They were won through the missionary work of Paul and others.

Paul was a Diaspora Jew reportedly from the notable city of Tarsus (now in Turkey). He was an opponent of the Jesus Followers until he had a religious experience with the resurrected Jesus which led him to join them. He turned from being a "Pharisee of Pharisees," that is, a strict practitioner of the Jewish religion, to being "all things to all men" in order to win them to the Jesus Way. He concluded that the Jewish laws were unnecessary for followers of Jesus. He turned from the human action of meticulously keeping the Law in order to be pleasing to God, to trusting in Jesus as the Messiah for justification by God's own action.

Paul was very successful in bringing Gentiles into a trusting relationship with Jesus/God. Paul called converts to the Way, "saints," or "disciples of Christ," or in the aggregate "churches of Christ." He evangelized mainly in Asia Minor,

Greece, and Macedonia. His activities and adventures are described in the New Testament book of Acts and in his own letters.

Gentile Christianity generally followed the order of Jewish and Hellenistic varieties. Members met regularly in assembly, probably daily at first, then finally on the first day of the week (Sunday). They met for fellowship, teaching, prayers, and common meals. They practiced baptism for converts. They may have been the first to transform the "breaking of bread" into a ritual.

Gentile Christians also were like the others in that they expected the soon return of Jesus to establish the Kingdom of God on Earth. Paul himself expected to be alive when Jesus returned. He expected that persons in the Kingdom would have spiritual/eternal bodies in order to experience a blessed existence beyond description.

This variety of Christianity flourished. Gentiles responded to the message of Paul and others in numbers that eclipsed those of the Jewish and Hellenistic varieties. With a modification of the belief in the soon return of Jesus, Gentile Christianity became the dominant variety of Christianity by the fourth century.

4. Apocalyptic Christianity.

If Jewish and Hellenistic Christianity are positioned on one side of Gentile Christianity, then Apocalyptic Christianity is positioned on the other side.

Apocalyptic Christianity arose because of the beliefs that Jesus would return soon and that God had to intervene in human history in order to establish the Kingdom; plus the factor of the persecution of Christians. When conditions became painful, even unbearable, in this world, then hope for an apocalyptic deliverance increased.

Apocalyptic Christianity flourished especially in Asia Minor. One of the earliest centers was at Hierapolis where the leader was Papias.

Another center was at Phrygia. The Christians there concluded that this world as it stood was not the true home of Christians. They separated themselves from regular society, met in the mountains, and prayed for the soon coming of Jesus. Montanus, and two women, Priscilla and Maximilla, were among the leaders. They proclaimed that Jesus would return soon and establish a New Jerusalem in Phrygia at a site called "Ardabau" near the cities of Pepuza and Tymion. These Christians prophesied, spoke in tongues, and went into trances. They attributed their ecstatic actions to the Holy Spirit, even as the ancient Jewish prophet Joel had promised and as Peter proclaimed on the day of Pentecost. They attracted large numbers of adherents throughout the Empire.

Apocalyptic Christians refused to show allegiance to the Roman Empire—they thought it was evil beyond redemption—and so were opposed to and opposed by the authorities. This stance also set them in opposition to Jewish, Hellenistic, and Gentile varieties of Christianity in which the leaders were trying to live amicably, if not always submissively, with Roman governments. The Apocalyptic Christians at Rome, Hierapolis, and Sardis were branded as "false prophets" by some of the bishops of the Gentile churches. On the other hand, they were praised by the noted Gentile Christian writers Tertullian and Irenaeus.

Apocalyptic Christians spawned many local churches. Congregations are noted in historical records in Judea in 198, in Syria in 202, and in Pontus about the same time. In 212 Tertullian himself joined them. Apocalyptic Christianity continued to be popular until the conversion of Constantine the Great in the early fourth century. When he became a Christian and stopped the persecution of Christians, then the radical message of the Apocalyptists was rendered null. A few Apocalyptists refused to give up, but Constantine ordered them to blend into mainstream Christianity, or be prosecuted.

In time this variety of Christianity was relegated to a minority; but a scant manifestation of it persisted.

5. Gnostic Christianity.

The Gnostic variety of Christianity can be placed on the same side of Gentile Christianity as the Apocalyptic variety, except farther out.

Gnostic Christianity was based on concepts of Jesus such as those recorded in The Gospel According to John. John mentioned both the divine and the human natures of Jesus, but it was the divine nature on which the Gnostics concentrated.

This variety of Christianity flourished in Alexandria and was present in a number of other locales.

Gnostic Christians believed that Jesus was the Messiah, just as did the other Christians. They went beyond the Apocalyptic Christians who had labeled this world as evil; they took evil to the cosmic level.

One way to describe their position is to see it from their point of view. God is purely good. The farther anything is from God, the less good it is. Also, God is pure spirit. This makes anything material less than God/good. Consequently, Jesus were actually material flesh he could not be fully divine, nor fully good, nor fully spirit. Because Jesus was good/spirit/God, Jesus could not have been conceived as human tissue in the human body of Mary and could not have been born in human flesh. Furthermore, God lives eternally. God is immortal. Jesus, being divine, could not have died on the cross because God does not die.

One of the sub-groups of Gnostic Christianity, the Docetists, believed that Jesus was only an apparition who appeared on Earth for the sake of communicating the divine mysteries. Jesus had the appearance of a human body only so that he could communicate; but he was not actually present in any material/fleshly/Earthly sense.

Early leaders of Gnostic Christianity were Valentinus of Rome (fl. 135-165), Ptolemy, and Basilides. In keeping with their theology, they described sin as a cosmological condition, not merely a catalog of Earthly errors. They believed that salvation lay in becoming "new creatures" in Christ. Salvation lay in knowing the truth, uniting in spirit with Christ, and following the good Jesus.

Gnostic churches flourished in the second century, but were opposed by the centrist stream of Christians. They were opposed also by Emperor Constantine in the fourth century. His imperial stance and the opposition of other Christians put Gnostic Christianity on the wane.

6. Marcionite Christianity.

Marcion of Rome about the year 140 CE began a distinct variety of Christianity. He used Greek, Jewish, Pauline, and Lukan literature to compose his variety.

In Greek literature, Plato had posed the question: "Is it good because the gods do it? Or do the gods do it because it is good?" Marcion went for the latter: good is that which even divinity must follow.

In Jewish literature the God led wars and on occasion was wrathful and murderous. Hence God in these ways was evil. On the other hand, Jesus always was good. Marcion opted for Jesus.

Pauline and Lukan literature pictured Jesus as the portrayal of the divinity who was good. Therefore, out with the God of the Bible (Old Testament) and in with the Jesus-like God.

Marcion accepted the theological implication that there must be two divinities, one evil and one good. The evil God must have created the world, since the world has sin in it and is not all good. The good God must be the redeemer of the world and the exemplar of righteousness. The rejected God is a demiurge who exudes evil. The accepted God is the savior who exudes good.

Marcion financed the collecting of Paul's and Luke's literature which he donated to the church in Rome. The church accepted it, but expelled Marcion because of his theological dualism.

Marcion himself imitated the compassionate way of Jesus and was morally exemplary. He was ascetic in his life-style, even though he was very wealthy—his riches came from his ownership of a maritime fleet of ships.

Marcion founded many local churches which lasted for centuries.

Women Named in the New Testament

1. Anna Lk. 2:36
2. Bernice Acts 25:13,23; 26:30
3. Candace Acts 8:27
4. Chloe 1 Cor. 1:11
5. Claudia 2 Tim. 4:21
6. Damaris Acts 17:34
7. Dorcas/Tabitha Acts 9:36,39,40
8. Drusilla Acts 24:24
9. Elizabeth Lk. 1:5,7,13,24,36,40,41,57
10. Eunice 2 Tim. 1:5
11. Euodia Philip. 4:2
12. Herodias Mt. 14:3,6; Mk. 6:17,19,22; Lk. 3:19
13. Joanna Lk. 8:3; 24:10
14. Julia Rom. 16:15
15. Junia Rom. 16:7
16. Lois 2 Tim. 1:5
17. Lydia Acts 16:14,40
18. Martha Lk. 10:38,40,41; Jn. 11:1,5,19,20, 21,24, 30,39; 12:2

There are several Marys and it is not always possible to know which is which; following is an approximation:

19. Mary Magdalene Mt. 27:56,61; 28:1; Mk. 15:40, 47; 16:1; Lk. 8:2; 24:10; Jn. 19:25; 20:1,11, 16,18
20. Mary, mother of James Mt. 27:56; Mk. 15:40; 16:1; Lk. 24:10
21. Mary, mother of Jesus Mt. 1:16,18,20; 2:11; 13:55; 27:56; Mk. 6:3; 15:40,47; Lk. 1:27, 30,34,38,39,41,46,56; 2:5,16,19,34; Acts 1:14
22. Mary, mother of John Acts 12:12
23. Mary, mother of Joses Mk. 15:47
24. Mary, of Rome Rom. 16:6

25. Mary, sister of Martha Lk. 10:39,42; Jn. 11:1,2, 19,20,28,31,32,45; 12:3
26. Mary, the other Mt. 27:61; 28:1
27. Mary, wife of Clopas Jn. 19:25
28. Nympha Col. 4:15
29. Phoebe Rom. 16:1
30. Priscilla/Prisca Acts 18:2,18,26; Rom. 16:3; 1 Cor. 16:19; 2 Tim. 4:19
31. Salome Mt. 15:40; 16:1
32. Sapphira Acts 5:1
33. Susanna Lk. 8:3
34. Syntyche Philip. 4:2
35. Tryphaena Rom. 16:12
36. Tryphosa Rom. 16:12

Glossary

Adonai – Hebrew for "my Lord"; a substitute name for YHWH/God, used only during prayer or Bible reading

Advent – the coming to Earth of Christ; later made part of the Christmas festival as a four week time of preparation for coming of Christ

Allegory – symbolic expression of meaning

Aphorism – short, pithy sayings, sometimes unconventional

Apocalypse – a threatening or destructive situation; purported revealing of future

Apocrypha – literature about final or catastrophic times; composed during times of ill fortune

Apology – justification, usually written, for a faith stance; treatises written by Christians in 2d and 3d centuries to justify Christianity to Roman officials

Apostle – title applied to Jesus' twelve disciples, to Paul, and to a few others in New Testament times; an ambassador

Apothegm – a brief unit of writing, aka pericope

Aramaic – everyday language in Israel in Jesus' day

Asceticism – rigorous denial of material or bodily comforts for sake of spiritual growth

Atonement – satisfying of an obligation; in Christian doctrine, the sacrifice of Jesus for human sin that satisfies the expectation of God

BCE/CE – "Before the Common Era,"/"Common Era"; contemporary designation of older BC/AD

Baptism – immersion in water as initiatory rite into Christianity; also practiced in various forms in other religions

Beatitudes – blessings listed in Matt. 5 and Lk. 6
Bible – sacred writings, composed of Old Testament for Jews, both Old and New Testaments for Christians; some sects add a few other works not in Old or New Testaments
Bishop – spiritual overseer; aka elder, presbyter
Blasphemy – unorthodox religious claims
Calvary – site of crucifixion of Jesus, probably a hill outside but near the walls of Jerusalem; aka Golgotha/Skull
Canon – officially approved writings
Catholic – universal; term not applied to church at Rome until c. 600 CE by Gregory I
Chanukkah – Jewish festival of liberation of Temple from Syrian rule in 165 BCE; 25th of Kislev (Nov/Dec)
Chapter – division inserted into a book for study and reference purposes; inserted in Bible probably in 13th century
Christ – anointed leader, usually a king, prophet, or high priest; applied as title to Jesus by Christians; equivalent of Hebrew "Messiah"
Christian – probably nickname for Christ Jesus followers in Antioch; later adopted by Christ followers as main name
Christmas – celebration of the birth of Jesus; not observed until second century, then set on January 6; in fourth century set on December 25 to upstage celebration in Mithraism of lengthening of the days and/or the celebration of Natalis Solis Invictus/Sol Invictus – sun's win over darkness
Christology – study of nature of Jesus
Church/House Church – persons who worship Jesus; "church" early referred to people, later to people and/or building; no buildings known until 3d century—people met in houses
Circumcision – trimming back of penis foreskin; for Jews sign of belonging to their ethnic group
Confession – statement of faith in Jesus

Covenant – agreement; several in Bible between God and Israel, such as Abrahamic, Mosaic, Davidic, Jeremiahic Covenants

Creed – statement of beliefs

Crucifixion – means of capital punishment by hanging condemned on a tree or cross, a painful and lengthy process of suffocation

Deacon – junior official of church; probably successor to servers who oversaw distribution of food and/or funds as mentioned in book of The Acts of the Apostles

Deuterocanon – books not universally recognized for inclusion in Bible, but important for history and instruction

Diaspora – Jews living outside Israel

Disciple – follower, learner

Docetic – belief that Jesus was completely spiritual, not material, prompted by belief that God was completely spiritual, hence anything material/fleshly was less than fully divine, hence tainted and sinful

Dualism – two realms of power: spirit and matter, light and dark, good and evil, YHWH and Devil, *et al*

Elder – senior official of church responsible for spiritual leadership; aka bishop, presbyter

Epistle – written correspondence, usually longer and on more serious subjects than letter

Eschatology – study of future and/or end times on grand scale

Essene – Jew living in desert area east and south of Jerusalem from about 160 BCE-70 CE; apocalyptic, ascetic, puritanical; thought main stream Judaism had forsaken true religion; may have hidden "Dead Sea Scrolls"

Eucharist – ceremony of thanksgiving, usually includes ritual of Lord's Supper/Communion

Evangelist – proclaimer of Gospel or other good news, usually parapatetic

Expiation – making right, especially to God, by sacrifice or ritual
Faith – trust; assent to doctrine
Forgiveness – clearing of indebtedness
Fornication – extra-marital sex
Gehenna/Gehinom – place of darkness and void where souls of wicked are punished and/or purified; associated with Valley Ben Hinnom south of Jerusalem where child sacrifices had been made to god Moloch
Gemara – commentary on Mishnah; incorporated into Talmud
Gentile – anyone not a Jew
Gnostic – belief in radical separation of good/spirit/God and evil/matter or flesh/Satan; salvation via specially revealed knowledge of separation resulting in return to fullness of God
Gospel – good news about Jesus
Grace – God's action of good will
Greek/Koine – language/dialect *lingua franca* in Mediterranean world and of New Testament
Hades – Greek term for underworld of the dead, often located in or below sea; aka Sheol, Gehenna
Hanukkah – see Chanukkah
Heaven – celestial abode of God; highest state of after-life
Hebrew – descendent of Abraham, later called Israelite/Jew; language of Abraham and descendents
Hell – abode of the unrighteous in after-life
Hellenism – mode of civilization instituted by Alexander the Great, synthesis of best features of Western societies
Heretic – one who holds to beliefs not catholic/universal or orthodox/correct
Herodian – one who was of family of or supported dynasty of Herod the Great
High Priest – highest Temple officer and spiritual authority in Israel
Holy Spirit – presence of God in human events; aka Advocate/Paraclete/Holy Ghost
Hypocrite – one who professes but doesn't practice
Incarnation – divinity become flesh

Jesus Followers – an early name for the Jesus movement
Jew – name for Hebrew/Israelite after Babylonian Exile in 6th century BCE
Judaism – name for Hebrew/Israelite/Jewish religion, probably first used after Babylonian Exile in 6th century BCE
Judgment/Day of Judgment/Day of the Lord – end time when God determines who is good and who is evil, rewards or punishes each
Justification – made right with God, by means such as grace or works or belief or faith
Kingdom of God – realm wherein God rules, either in Heaven or on Earth; usually a future hoped-for realm, although some Christians claimed it had come with Jesus and/or church
Kingdom of Heaven – usual Jewish term for Kingdom of God, but sometimes of lesser status than Kingdom of God
Kosher/Kashrut – Jewish food laws
Lamb of God – applied to Jesus by those who thought he was perfect sacrifice for sin
Logos – rational principle of universe; translated from Greek as "word"/"reason"/"expression"; applied by The Gospel According to John to Jesus
Lord's Supper – last supper Jesus and his disciples shared before crucifixion, during which Christians believed ritual of Communion was instituted
Martyr – one who witnesses to or dies for faith
Messiah – anointed one; God's representative for special work such as king, prophet, or high priest; fully human until Christian doctrine of divinity of Jesus; equivalent of Greek "Christ"
Midrash – commentary on sacred writings
Mikveh – Jewish rite of immersion in water for the cleansing ceremony of tevilah
Miracle – supernatural interruption of natural laws
Monotheism – belief in one and only one God

Mystery Religion/s – religion/s in Gentile world which claimed special revelations from divinity, observed purification rituals similar to baptism, partook of sacred meals, and promised that union with divinity/apotheosis would carry them finally into eternal, ideal, heavenly life
Myth – a non-true story that carries truth
Nazarene – one specially dedicated to God, signified outwardly by not cutting one's hair or drinking wine
Nazarenes – an early name for the Jesus movement
New Testament – sacred scriptures of Christianity
Novella – literary designation for Biblical material of historical novel type: story plus moral
Office – authoritative position in church
Old Testament – sacred scriptures of Jews who call it Bible/Tenakh; also claimed as sacred but secondary by Christians
Oral Law/Tradition – development of Mosaic Law in speech or discussion rather than in writing
Orthodox – correct, right, dominant
Orthopraxy – correct/right/dominant practice
Pagan – originally an Italian farmer, later one not Jew or Christian
Paraclete – see Holy Spirit
Parousia – end time presence or second coming of Jesus or establishment of Kingdom of God
Passion – last week of Jesus' life; or event of Jesus giving his life on cross; suffering
Passover – Jewish festival commemorating Exodus of Israel from bondage in Egypt; 14th of Nisan (Mar/Apr); time of crucifixion of Jesus
Pax Romana – Peace of Rome; special concern Rome had for tranquil society
Pentecost – Jewish festival commemorating giving of Law to Moses at Mt. Sinai; 6th, 7th Sivan (May/Jun); occasion in 29/30 CE when church started
Pericope – see apothegm

Pharisee – one of Jewish party devoted to religious purity and scholarship in Law
Phylactery – small pouch containing Bible passages, worn on forehead and left arm during prayers by Jews
Pilgrimage – journey; journey to religion site
Pleroma – fullness; favored term by Gnostic Christians to denote completeness of divinity
Pneumatology – study of or doctrine of Holy Spirit
Prayer – a depth experience with ultimate reality
Predestinaton – pre-arranged fate by divinity
Prefect – Roman official of equestrian rank, similar to governor or proconsul; rulers in Judea 6-41 CE
Presbyter – spiritual leader of church; aka elder/bishop
Proconsul – Roman official just superior to prefect, aka governor
Proto-Orthodox – nascent dominant Christianity
Pseudepigrapha – works ascribed to another, written 200 BCE-200 CE, read for history and instruction but not recognized by all as canonical
Reconciliation – bringing the estranged back together, as of God and humans
Redemption – buying back of that which was given over to or taken over by another or by sin
Repentance – sorrow for sin and intention not to sin again
Resurrection – was dead, now is alive
Revelation – knowledge given by divinity to humanity
Righteousness – being in accord with God, or doing God's will
Sabbath – Jewish holy day, from sundown Friday to sundown Saturday
Sadducee – one of Jewish aristocratic party, strict constructionist of Law
Saint – member of church; later singled out as particularly good member of church
Salvation – freedom from evil and freedom to righteousness; deliverance from God's wrath and receiving of eternal bliss

Samaritan – resident of Samaria, in Jesus' time of mixed blood, believed by Jews to be inferior because not fully Jewish by blood or religion; one of small remnant of Samaritans claiming heritage from Abraham

Sanctification – process of making holy, acceptable to God

Sanhedrin – highest Jewish council headed by high priest

Satan – name for a divinity, at first not evil but a kind of investigator/prosecutor, later tempter/evil one/devil/adversary; origin of demiurge aspect probably came into Judaism from Zoroastrianism

Savior – one who rescues from danger

Scribe – Jewish lawyer; one able to read and write

Second Coming – reappearance of Jesus on Earth to set up Kingdom of God or sweep faithful into Heaven

Septuagint – Greek version of Jewish Bible, translated in 3d and 2d centuries BCE; aka LXX (Seventy)

Sicarii – small subset of Zealot party ready to kill any Roman or Jewish collaborator with Romans, even at sacrifice of own life

Sin – disobedience or distrust of God, estrangement from God

Son of God – faithful Hebrew/Jew; in Christianity applied to Jesus as being divine

Son of Man – special emissary from God, usually divine

Soteriology – study of or doctrine of salvation

Spiritual Gifts – New Testament term for leadership and ministering endowments from Holy Spirit

Synagogue – Jewish, both the people and the building in which they met for study, prayer, and fellowship

Synoptic – seeing as with one eye, applied to the similar Gospels According to Mark, Matthew, and Luke

Talmud – comprehensive designation for collection of Jewish oral law and commentary

Tanakh – more recent term for Jewish Bible; acronym for Torah/Law, Nevi'im/Prophets, and Khetubim/Writings

Targum – Aramaic translation of Hebrew scriptures

Temple – great shrine of Jews in Jerusalem for worship of and sacrifice to God; twice destroyed in war; not rebuilt since 70 CE

Testament – covenant; collections of scriptures in Bible

Tevilah – Jewish ceremony of cleansing with water

Theodicy – human attempt to explain and justify actions perceived to be performed by divinity

Torah – Jewish term for Law of Moses; teaching, instruction

Traditional Religion/s – religion/s associated with beginning of civilizations or societies; primarily concerned with help for living in this world rather than the hereafter

Tribune – Roman judge usually with limited power to punish

Verse – a division inserted into chapter of book for ease of study and reference; inserted in Bible by Verus Stephanus in 1551 CE

Way – an early name for the Jesus movement

YHWH – early name for God, usually assigned vowels to form Yahweh; also translated as "Jehovah" according to German pronunciation

Zealot – one of Jewish freedom party willing to fight and/or kill any and all usurpers of Jewish rights

Bibliography

Bainton, Roland H. *Christendom: A Short History of Christianity and Its Impact on Western Civilization.* Volume I. *From the Birth of Christ to the Reformation.* New York: Harper Torchbooks, The Cloister Library, Harper & Row, Publishers, 1964. 274 pages. Illustrations. Bibliography. Index.

Blackburn, Simon. *The Oxford Dictionary of Philosophy.* Oxford: Oxford University Press, 1994. 408 pages. Appendix: Logical Symbols.

Boer, Harry R. *A Short History of the Early Church.* Grand Rapids, Michigan: William B. Eerdmans Publishing Company, 1976. 184 pages. Bibliography. Index.

Borg, Marcus J. *Reading the Bible Again for the First Time: Taking the Bible Seriously but Not Literally.* San Francisco: Harper, 2002. 321 pages. Indices: Subject, Modern Author, Scripture.

Brown, Raymond E., and John P. Meier. *Antioch and Rome: New Testament Cradles of Catholic Christianity.* New York: Paulist Press, 1983. 242 pages. Bibliography. Indices: Bibliographic, Subject.

Browning, W.R.F. *A Dictionary of the Bible.* New York: Oxford University Press, 1996. 407 pages. Maps. Appendices: Measures, Weights, Coinage, Dates. Bibliography.

Bibliography

Carmody, Denise Lardner, and John Tully Carmody. *Christianity: An Introduction.* 3d ed. Belmont, California: Wadsworth Publishing Company, A Division of Wadsworth, Inc., 1995. 260 pages. Appendix: Membership of Major American Religious Groups, 1990. Glossary. Bibliography. Index.

Coogan, Michael D. *The Oxford History of the Biblical World.* Oxford: Oxford University Press, 1998. 487 pages. Illustrations. Chronologies. Maps. Bibliographies. Index.

Cory, Catherine A., and David T. Landry, eds. *The Christian Theological Tradition.* Needham Heights, Massachusetts: Simon & Schuster Custom Publishing, 1996. 435 pages. Illustrations. Maps. Glossary. Index.

Crossan, John Dominic, and Jonathan L. Reed. *Excavating Jesus: Beneath the Stones, Behind the Texts.* San Francisco: Harper, A Division of Harper Collins Publishers, 2001. 298 pages. Illustrations. Maps. Bibliography. Index.

Cunningham, Phillip J. *A Believer's Search for the Jesus of History.* New York/Mahwah, New Jersey: Paulist Press, 1999. 154 pages. Bibliography.

Dowley, Tim, ed. *Introduction to the History of Christianity.* Rev. ed. Minneapolis: Fortress Press, 1995. First publ. 1977. Illustrations. Maps. Chronologies. Indices: People, Places, Subjects, Bible References, Pictures.

Dunn, James D.G. *The Partings of the Ways: Between Christianity and Judaism and Their significance for the Character of Christianity.* London and Philadelphia: SCM Press and Trinity Press International, 1991. 368 pages. Appendix: Unity and Diversity in the Church. Bibliography. Indices: Biblical and Ancient Writings, Modern Authors, Subject.

Ehrman, Bart D. *A Brief Introduction to the New Testament.* New York: Oxford University Press, 2004. 380 pages. Illustrations. Maps. Chronology. Glossary. Index.

Ehrman, Bart D. *Lost Christianities: The Battles for Scripture and the Faiths We Never Knew.* Oxford: Oxford University Press, 2003. 294 pages. Illustrations. Chronology. Bibliography. Index.

Ehrman, Bart D. *Lost Scriptures: Books that Did Not Make It into the New Testament.* Oxford: Oxford University Press, 2003. 342 pages. Canonical Lists.

Ehrman, Bart D. *The New Testament and Other Early Christian Writings: A Reader.* 2d ed. New York: Oxford University Press, 2004. 419 pages.

Ehrman, Bart D. *The New Testament: A Historical Introduction to the Early Christian Writings.* 3d ed. New York: Oxford University Press, 2004. 506 pages. Ilustrations. Maps. Time Lines. Glossary. Bibliographies. Index.

Eusebius. *The History of the Church from Christ to Constantine.* Transl. G.A. Williamson. Baltimore: Penguin Books, 1965. First publ. c. 325. 429 pages. Appendices: Emperors and Bishops, Bishoprics, Martyrdoms, Heretics, Sources Quoted or Summarized, Canon of the New Testament. Index.

Ferguson, Everett. *Backgrounds of Early Christianity.* Grand Rapids, Michigan: William B. Eerdmans Publishing Company, 1987. Bibliography. Indices: Subject, Scripture.

Flanders, Henry Jackson, Jr., and Robert Wilson Crapps, David Anthony Smith. *People of the Covenant: An Introduction to the Hebrew Bible.* 4th ed. New York: Oxford University Press, 1996. 562 pages. Illustrations. Chronology. Maps. Glossary. Bibliography. Index.

Grant, Robert M. *Augustus to Constantine: The Rise and Triumph of Christianity in the Roman World.* San Francisco: Harper & Row, Publishers, 1970. 334 pages. Appendix: Roman Emperors and Bishops. Bibliography. Index.

Harris, Stephen L. *Understanding the Bible.* 4th ed. Mountain View, California: Mayfield Publishing Company, 1997. 558 pages. Illustrations. Tables. Maps. Glossary. Bibliographies. Index.

Hastings, Adrian, and Alistair Mason, Hugh Pyper, eds., with Ingrid Lawrie and Cecily Bennett. *The Oxford Companion to Christian Thought: Intellectual, Spiritual, and Moral Horizons of Christianity.* Oxford: Oxford University Press, 2000. 777 pages. Index: Persons without entries.

Hill, Brennan. *Jesus the Christ: Contemporary Perspectives.* Mystic, Connecticut: Twenty-Third Publications, 2d printing 1992. Bibliography. Indices: Scripture Citations, Subject.

Hinson, E. Glenn. *The Early Church: Origins to the Dawn of the Middle Ages.* Nashville: Abingdon Press, 1996. 365 pages. Bibliography.

Isaacson, Ben. *Dictionary of the Jewish Religion.* David Gross, ed. Saul Teplitz, preface. New York: Bantam Books, 1979. 196 pages. Illustrations. Appendices: Hebrew Alphabet, Days, Months, Holidays and Festivals, Chronology, Population, Modern Israel's Government. Bibliography.

Johnson, Paul. *A History of Christianity.* New York: Atheneum, 1979. 556 pages. Bibliography. Index.

Kee, Howard Clark, and Emily Albu, Carter Lindberg, J. William Frost, Dana L. Robert. *Christianity: A Social and Cultural History.* 2d ed. Upper Saddle River, New Jersey: Prentice Hall, 1998. 600 pages. Bibliography. Index.

Kee, Howard Clark. *Understanding the New Testament.* 4th ed. Englewood Cliffs, New Jersey: Prentice-Hall, Inc., 1983. 408 pages. Chronology. Appendices: Life-World View and Historiography, Oral Forms in the Synoptic Gospels, Q Source, Literary Relationships among the "Prison Epistles," Authority Models in the Early Church. Index.

Lyda, Hap C.S. *History of Biblical Judaism: An Introductory Study of the Bible.* 5th ed. Fort Worth: 21st Century Press, 2d printing 2008. 272 pages. Tables. Maps. Appendices: Names for God, Monotheism, Theories on How the Bible Was Written, Bible Canon, Other Writings Mentioned in the Bible, Food, Jewish Calendar, Festivals, Timeline. Glossary. Bibliographies. Index.

Manschreck, Clyde L. *A History of Christianity in the World: From Persecution to Uncertainty.* Englewood Cliffs, New Jersey: Prentice-Hall, Inc., 1974. 378 pages. Bibliography. Index.

Matthews, Victor H. *Manners and Morals in the Bible.* Peabody, Massachusetts: Hendrickson Publishers, 1988. 283 pages. Illustrations. Maps. Bibliography. Indices: Subject, Names, Places, Ancient Texts.

McGiffert, Arthur Cushman. *A History of Christian Thought.* Volume I. *Early and Eastern: From Jesus to John of Damascus.* New York: Charles Scribner's Sons, 1932. 352 pages. Bibliography. Index.

McGrath, Alister E. *An Introduction to Christianity.* Cambridge, Massachusetts: Blackwell Publishers, 1997. 444 pages. Illustrations. Glossary. Bibliography. Index.

McManners, John, ed. *The Oxford Illustrated History of Christianity.* Oxford: Oxford University Press, 1992. 724 pages. Illustrations. Chronology. Maps. Bibliography. Index.

Metzger, Bruce M., and Michael D. Coogan, eds. *The Oxford Guide to People & Places of the Bible.* Oxford: Oxford University Press, 2001. 374 pages. Maps. Bibliography. Index.

Metzger, Bruce M., and Michael D. Coogan. *The Oxford Companion to the Bible.* New York: Oxford University Press, 1993. 874 pages. Maps. Bibliography. Index.

Metzger, Bruce M., and Michael D. Coogan. *The Oxford Guide to Ideas & Issues of the Bible.* Oxford: Oxford University Press, 2001. 585 pages. Bibliography. Index.

Metzger, Bruce Manning. *The New Testament: Its Background, Growth, and Content.* 2d ed. Nashville: Abingdon Press, 1983. 309 pages. Maps. Appendices: Formation of the Canon of the New Testament, Transmission and Translation of the Bible. Bibliographies. Indices: New Testament References, General.

Newsome, James D. *Greeks, Romans, Jews: Currents of Culture and Belief in the New Testament World.* Philadelphia: Trinity Press International, 1992. 475 pages. Charts. Maps. Bibliography. Index.

Nystrom, Bradley P., and David P. Nystrom. *The History of Christianity: An Introduction.* Boston: McGraw Hill, 2004. 414 pages. Illustrations. Glossary. Bibliography. Index.

Puskas, Charles B. *An Introduction to the New Testament.* Peabody, Massachusetts: Hendrickson Publishers, 1989. 297 pages. Illustrations. Charts. Maps. Appendices: Formation of New Testament Canon, English Translations of the New Testament. Indices: Ancient Texts, Authors.

Reicke, Bo. *The New Testament Era: The World of the Bible from 500 B.C. to A.D. 100.* Transl. David E. Green. Philadelphia: Fortress Press, 1968. First publ. 1964. 336 pages. Maps. Bibliography. Index.

Sawyer, Deborah F. *Women and Religion in the First Christian Centuries.* New Fetter Lane, London: Routledge, 1996. 186 pages. Bibliography. Index.

Spivey, Robert A., and D. Moody Smith. *Anatomy of the New Testament: A Guide to Its Structure and Meaning.* 5th ed. Englewood Cliffs, New Jersey: Prentice Hall, 1995. 513 pages. Illustrations. Charts. Chronology. Maps. Glossary. Bibliography. Indices: Name and Subject, Biblical Passages.

Stambaugh, John E., and David L. Balch. *The New Testament in Its Social Environment. Library of Early Christianity.* Wayne A. Meeks, ed. Philadelphia: The Westminster Press, 1986. 194 pages. Maps. Bibliography. Indices: Subjects, New Testament Passages.

Walker, Williston. *A History of the Christian Church.* Revised ed. by Cyril C. Richardson, Wilhelm Pauck, and Robert T. Handy. New York: Charles Scribner's Sons, 1959. First publ. 1918. 585 pages. Maps. Bibliography. Index.

Weaver, Mary Jo. *Introduction to Christianity.* 2d ed. Belmont, California: Wadsworth Publishing Company, A Division of Wadsworth, Inc., 1991. 310 pages. Appendices: Order of books in Old Testament, Synopsis of Books of Old and New Testaments, Early Christian Writers, Ecumenical Councils, Creeds and Confessions, Church Structure and Polity, Historical Time Line. Glossary. Bibliographies. Index.

Witherington, Ben III. *Women and the Genesis of Christianity.* Ann Witherington, ed. Cambridge: University Press, 1990. 273 pages. Bibliography. Index: Scripture Citations.

Yamauchi, Edwin. *Harper's World of the New Testament.* San Francisco: Harper & Row, Publishers, 1981. 128 pages. Illustrations. Charts. Maps.

Zahl, Paul F.M. *The First Christian: Universal Truth in the Teachings of Jesus.* Grand Rapids, Michigan: William B. Eerdmans Publishing Company, 2003. 138 pages. Bibliography. Indices: Authors, Bible References.

Index

Index